POLIT
REVOLUTION
IN THE
REFORMED TRADITION

POLITICAL REVOLUTION

IN THE
REFORMED TRADITION

A HISTORICAL AND BIBLICAL CRITIQUE

SAM WALDRON

FREE GRACE PRESS

Published by

Free Grace Press
3900 Dave Ward Dr., Ste. 1900
Conway, AR 72034
(501) 214-9663
email: support@freegracepress.com
website: www.freegracepress.com

Printed in the United States of America

ISBN: 978-1-952599-49-1

For additional Reformed Baptist titles, please email us for a free list or see our website at the above address.

Presented to the faculty of Grand Rapids Baptist Seminary in fulfillment of the requirements for the ThM Degree

CONTENTS

—

Introduction

I want to thank Free Grace Press for publishing my Master of Theology thesis and Liz Smith for her work on my tome. I wrote this thesis about thirty-five years ago for what was then Grand Rapids Baptist Seminary. My chief advisor was Dr. Jim Grier, whose memory and instruction I remember with great thankfulness.

This book, then, was not written during the COVID-19 pandemic. In that sense, it does not address any of the wild and contradictory currents rushing through the church in recent years with reference to the church's relation to civil government. But though this thesis was not written in light of any of these movements, I did seek to have it published recently because I think that its thesis and arguments have taken on new relevance in light of the many puzzling questions COVID and the COVID mandates have confronted the church and its pastors.

The thesis just mentioned is that violent, political revolution is both a violation of the Scriptures and a contradiction of the teaching of the historical fount of the Reformed tradition, John Calvin. Several comments about this thesis and its significance may serve to attract the reader to this volume.

First, I do not hold the "Calvin versus the Calvinists" motif so popular with a previous generation of church historians. That thesis was a massively inflated view of the theological developments that took place after Calvin's life and ministry and the doctrinal distinctions between Calvin and his successors.

Second, that thesis, as I have just suggested, is not without an element of truth. It is unquestionable there are certain differences between Calvin and his successors. One of them is that Calvin rejected violent revolution. He is not the author—in fact, he is the adversary—of that tradition as it developed in the Reformed tradition. William Cunningham (1805–1861) cannot be accused of being influenced by twentieth-century historiography. Yet he cautions against wrongly flattening the difference between Calvin and his successors. He has this to say about Calvin and the Calvinists:

> And it has often been alleged that Beza, in his very able discussions of this subject, carried his views upon some points farther than Calvin himself did, so that he has been described as being *Calvino Calvinior*. We are not prepared to deny altogether the truth of this allegation; but we are persuaded that there is less ground for it than is sometimes supposed, and that the points of alleged difference between them in matters of doctrine, respect chiefly topics on which Calvin was not led to give any very formal or explicit deliverance, because they were not at the time subjects of discussion, or indeed ever present to his thoughts.[1]

Third, crucial to my argument in this thesis is that we must make a clear and important distinction between the civil situation in the theocratic kingdom of Israel and the one in which we live today under the Gentile kingdoms. This means that bringing into the current debates about civil government proof-texts that assume the civil situation in the Old Testament theocracy is quite misleading. In that situation, there was a somewhat different relation of the people of God to the civil ruler than there is today.

Fourth, I think this distinction between the Old Testament theocracy and our situation under the Gentile kingdoms is crucial to a right assessment of the revised and renewed emphasis on "theonomy" today. All too often, both historically in the Reformed tradition and in arguments for theonomy today, this crucial distinction is entirely forgotten.

---

1   William Cunningham, *The Reformers and the Theology of the Reformation*, 349–50.

Fifth, at first glance my argument against revolution may seem intended to support those who want to emphasize the Christian's duty to obey the government in almost everything. In fact, this reaction to the thesis of my book is wholly unjustified. Crucial to my thesis is the idea that Paul's call in Romans 13 is not "don't disobey the government." It is rather "don't become terrorists; don't join the Jewish revolution against Rome." To put it more positively, it is "be subordinate to Rome." It is not "obey everything they say." Obedience and subordination are often closely related, but they are two quite different things.

Sixth, and just to make what I am saying clear, with regard to obeying government, my view is this: there are times when the Christian must disobey the government (Acts 4:19, 20; 5:29). He *must* obey God rather than any human authority in cases where they conflict. It is also my view that the Christian *may* disobey the government where it exceeds its lawful jurisdiction and invades the jurisdiction of another divinely appointed human authority—like the jurisdiction of the church or family (Matt 22:21). My thesis is not an argument for a kind of servility to the civil authority.

All in all, I do think this book embodies a crucial perspective to guide the church and the Christian through the perplexing ethical questions that have descended upon us in our day. May God grant the light of His Word to shine through it and guide us to His holy hill!

Chapter 1

A Summary of the Question Addressed and the Argument Pursued in the Thesis

I. The Question Addressed

A. Stated

Given the normativity of the Scriptures for the state maintained both by the Reformed tradition and in the Scriptures themselves, does this entail the consequent of justifying under certain circumstances political revolution?

B. Explained

For the fuller understanding of both the relevance and meaning of the question addressed in this dissertation and stated above, several explanatory remarks must now be appended.

1. The doctrine of the political normativity of the Scriptures is not the thesis of this dissertation. It is its premise. It is assumed at the outset that the Reformed tradition is right in teaching the sovereignty of God and His inscripturated Word over the state. Though this assumption will unavoidably be supported both directly and indirectly in

this dissertation, a systematic statement of its supporting evidence is outside its scope and intention. Indeed, it is difficult to feel that such an assumption is in need of systematic advocacy.

2. Those who regard the moral norms of Scripture as authoritative for the state have disagreed on many of the specific out-workings of that position. Is the state responsible to punish violations of the "first table of the law?" Is the civil code of Israel intended as a model for all states? Is it possible to maintain the separation of church and state within the framework of the doctrine of the political normativity of the Scriptures? Each of these important questions have become the subject of renewed evaluation in our day and would require a separate dissertation to adequately address. Such questions are, however, not at issue in this dissertation.

3. The doctrine of just political revolution was advocated early and has been advocated frequently in the Reformed tradition. Zwingli himself is thought to have held it.[1] Evidence will be cited that suggests that large steps were being taken toward such a doctrine even in the era of Calvin by men such as Beza and Knox. It is classically and properly associated with Rutherford's *Lex Rex*.[2] This doctrine has surfaced again in the modern Reformed camp among theonomist circles and in the writings of Francis and Franky Schaeffer.[3] In more extreme form, it

---

1 John Howard Yoder, *The Politics of Jesus* (Grand Rapids: Eerdmans, 1972), 201.
2 Samuel Rutherford, *Lex Rex, or, the law and the prince: a dispute for the just prerogative of king and people . . .* (Harrisonburg, VA: Sprinkle, 1982).
3 Gary North, ed., *The Theology of Christian Resistance* (Tyler, TX: Geneva Divinity School Press, 1983), xvi, xx, 3–11, 51–64, 102–110, 237, 238, 288–295; Francis Schaeffer, *A Christian Manifesto* (Westchester, IL: Crossway, 1982), 67–132; Franky Schaeffer, *A Time for Anger: The Myth of Neutrality* (Crossway, Westchester, Illinois, 1982), 46–54, 122, 150.

has been advocated in certain of the modern Liberation theologies.[4]

4. It is not surprising that it is the Reformed tradition that has most often been associated with the doctrine of just revolution. That tradition has most pointedly emphasized the limitations of the state and its subordination to God Himself. Reformed theology explicitly rejected the state's claim to authority over the church and emphatically proclaimed the sovereignty of God over all things. This thoroughly rebuked the civil idolatry characteristic of human societies. In such an atmosphere and in view of the difficult political situations faced by the Reformed wing of Protestantism during the Reformation period, it was to be expected that some would draw the seemingly logical conclusion of the doctrine of just revolution. Thus, not unnaturally, the doctrine of just revolution has been generally identified with the Reformed tradition.

5. The phrase *political revolution* is a crucial one in this thesis and must be clearly defined. By it is meant violent resistance against an existing civil order by those subordinate to it.[5] In this definition the term *violent* is use of armed force or, as the Bible would put it, the taking up of the sword (Matt 26:52).

6. A keen awareness of the questions that may be raised by such a definition is felt. To some extent the demonstration of the historical and biblical propriety of this definition must await the evidence to be presented within the pages of this dissertation. Two comments are appropriate, however, in order to elucidate the meaning of the definition given above.

---

4   Yoder, *The Politics of Jesus*, 201.

5   Yoder defines *revolution* similarly. His definition had a distinct influence on the one given here. He says, "In this section I have taken 'rebellion' in the current sense of violent overthrow," 202.

7. A historical reference may serve to crystallize the precise intention and significance of this definition. Calvin, in one of the most discussed statements ever written by him, asserted:

> For though the correction of tyrannical domination is the vengeance of God, we are not, therefore, to conclude that it is committed to us, who have received no other command than to obey and suffer. This observation I always apply to private persons. For if there be in the present day any magistrates appointed for the protection of the people and the moderation of the power of kings, . . . I am so far from prohibiting them in the discharge of their duty to oppose the violence or cruelty of kings, that I affirm, that if they connive at kings in their oppression of their people, such forbearance involves the most nefarious perfidy, because such fraudulently betray the liberty of the people, of which they know that they have been appointed protectors by the ordination of God.[6]

The precise significance of this statement will be considered at length within the body of this dissertation. The point to be made here, however, is simply that armed opposition to the violence, tyranny, and cruelty of kings by such magistrates would not properly be called revolution. Serving under such magistrates in armed forces would not constitute rebellion. As Calvin explicitly remarks, such magistrates are themselves "protectors by the ordination of God." Such magistrates would by the provision of the civil order itself have a legitimate claim to civil authority— would-be the true, existing, civil authority—ordained of God.

Another comment is pertinent. In our definition, as also for Calvin and for the Scriptures, there is no question of

---

6   John Calvin, *The Institutes of the Christian Religion*, trans. by John Allen (Philadelphia, n. d.), 2:804 (4:20.31).

distinguishing between legitimate and illegitimate existing civil orders. Neither the origin, form, nor conduct of a civil order is relevant to the question of revolution against it. The existence alone—that is to say, the actual possession of ruling power, the power of the sword—by a civil order is sufficient to validate its right to the subordination of its subjects.

8. Within the Reformed tradition various positions have been taken by those holding to the doctrine of just revolution in regard to the following questions: (1) When is political revolution justified? and (2) Who may lead such revolutions? So long as political revolution as defined above is advocated, the precise variations in response to such questions are irrelevant for our thesis. For example, some Reformed writers have maintained that only civil magistrates may lead armed rebellion. The question to be asked is, simply, does the civil magistrate in question have the lawful right to do so within the existing civil order? If he does, he is not leading a rebellion or revolution according to the definition. If he does not, then no matter his exact position in that government, he is violating the biblical prohibition of revolution. Quite obviously, difficult and even ambiguous situations may in rare instances arise. This is the case in any area of ethics. Such situations must not be allowed to cloud the basic clarity of the biblical demands.

II. THE ARGUMENT PURSUED

The position that the doctrine of just revolution is necessitated by the Reformed doctrine that the Scriptures are normative for the state will be critiqued historically and biblically. Particularly, the historical but also to some extent the biblical critique of this position will be selective. An exhaustive survey of the positions of Reformed theologians over the last four centuries is simply not within the scope of this dissertation. Neither is it necessary for the demonstration of its thesis. It is hoped that the sufficiency of the selective historical critique as well as the sufficiency of the selective biblical critique of this position will be evident.

Historically, it will be shown that the central figure of the Reformed tradition, Calvin himself, rejected the doctrine of just revolution.

Biblically, it will be shown via an examination of a critical period in the Old Testament and a classic passage in the New Testament that the Bible nowhere deduces the doctrine of just revolution from the sovereignty of God and His Word and, in fact, by example and precept prohibits all political revolution properly so called. Perhaps it is with reference to the biblical critique that the most doubt may be entertained as to its sufficiency. It will become clear that the two foci of the biblical critique mentioned above will provide an adequate survey of the biblical teaching.

In the conclusion to this dissertation, the replies to significant objections to the thesis will be summarized. Also, the importance of the thesis will be underscored by its application to modern theories of just revolution gaining prominence in our day, to political ethics as a whole, and to social ethics in general. As this indicates, the conviction with which the demonstration of the thesis is undertaken is that the thesis is of broad significance for modern Christian ethics.

Before concluding this introduction to the thesis, it is appropriate to indicate the logical status or character of the critique it contains. It is addressed against those who would hold that the relation of the doctrine of the political normativity of the Scriptures to the doctrine of just revolution is that of an A-type categorical proposition. In other words, those who hold the view this thesis critiques say that the doctrine of the political normativity of the Scriptures logically requires the doctrine of just revolution (all S are P). The thesis of this dissertation is that this logical analysis is fallacious. It seeks to show that the relation is rather that of an O-type categorical proposition, which asserts that some S are not P. In other words, it seeks to demonstrate that the doctrine of the political normativity of the Scriptures does not logically require the conclusion of the doctrine of just revolution. Or, to change the logical framework, it seeks to show that the doctrine of the political normativity of the Scriptures is not a sufficient condition for the doctrine of just revolution. It seeks to show this through the presentation of historical and biblical evidence that even where the doctrine of the political normativity of the Scriptures is acknowledged, the doctrine of just revolution was rejected.

Part 1

THE HISTORICAL CRITIQUE

Chapter 2

CALVIN, REVOLUTION, AND THE SOCIAL CONTRACT THEORY

Vast, century-spanning debate has raged over the political commitments of John Calvin.[1] Damned as the "Tyrant of Geneva," he has been lauded as the "Founder of America."[2] It is the stated opinion of the writer, to be established in this chapter, that such diversity of judgment is due far more to the prejudices of Calvin's interpreters than to the teaching of Calvin himself. It may be that to some small degree the vigor of Calvin's language in preaching the Word of God may be responsible for the confusion. On the other hand, if the thesis of this paper is correct, it will tend to corroborate the view that few men have ever written so much, so well, so clearly, and indeed, so consistently as Calvin.[3]

The prejudices already mentioned have been occasioned, however, by two issues that one must confront in studying Calvin's political commitments. These prejudices are revealed first in our understanding of and attitude toward democracy. What do we understand democracy to be? What is our attitude

---

1   A. J. L. Waskey, "John Calvin's Theory of Political Obligation: An Examination of the Doctrine of Civil Obedience and Its Limits from the New Testament Commentaries" (University of Southern Mississippi, PhD, 1987), 32f.

2   R. M. Kingdon and R. D. Linder, eds., *Calvin and Calvinism: Sources of Democracy?* (Lexington, MA: Heath, 1970), 7.

3   Waskey, "John Calvin's Theory of Political Obligation," 32.

toward democracy? The way in which we answer such questions will profoundly affect our assessment of Calvin's political commitments as they relate to democracy. One has commented, "The main intention of most historians who try to resurrect the political ideology of John Calvin seems to be to either find the origins of modern freedom and republicanism on the one hand or the opposite of them on the other."[4] Most writers assume the undeniable success of the "American experiment in democracy." Hence, if they are sympathetic to Calvin and Calvinism, they have striven to claim them as the spring of American democracy. If they are not favorable to Calvin and Calvinism, they tend to picture him as hostile to such a political environment.

A related difficulty has already been implied. It is epitomized in such questions as these: What is Calvin and Calvinism? What do I think of them? Are the views of Calvin and, later, Calvinism the same in this matter? Did the views of Beza and the rest of Calvin's theological heirs seriously deviate from Calvin's on political matters? Such questions must, to some degree, be addressed when dealing with the issue this chapter is addressing.

The viewpoint of this treatment is that Calvin was neither hierocrat nor democrat but something other. While this chapter addresses itself to the latter of these views, for the sake of clarity, a word must be said about the former.

Was Calvin a hierocrat, a Protestant pope presiding over a Genevan theocracy? The term *theocracy* is itself ambiguous. The popular impression it conveys, however, is that of a hierocracy—that is, that Calvin was the political ruler of Geneva.[5] If this is what is meant by a Genevan theocracy, it is simply another part of the "Calvin legend" and a blatant and inexcusable historical falsehood. Its perpetuation by reputable historians is completely indefensible. Such nonsense as the following is not uncommon:

---

4   Ronald Vandermolen, "Political Calvinism," *The Journal of Church and State*, XI (1969), 457.

5   *Hierocracy* may be literally defined as the rule of a state by priests or clerics.

The Calvinist wing of Protestantism adopted a rather different political attitude. Its ideal of church independence was as pronounced as that of Catholicism; the theocracy which its founder, John Calvin (1509–1564), had established at the Swiss city of Geneva had completely subordinated secular government to the ecclesiastical authorities of the Calvinist church in a regime far more severe than that of the Medieval Catholic Church. "New presbyter is but old priest writ large," the English poet, John Milton, was to say a century later.[6]

Such half-truths betray an astounding ignorance of the most basic facts about Calvin's life and Geneva's government. Let reputable Calvin scholars refute such foolishness. Marc Cheneviere is well-known for his exploding of this myth.

Some illusions are extremely difficult to dispel! Even today many Protestants imagine that the ideal politico-religious regime of Calvinism is a theocracy, understanding by that term a political regime which implies the domination of the clergy over civil society. In actual fact, however, no notion could be more erroneous; Calvin never showed the least sympathy for a political regime of this sort, in proof of which statement may be cited his constant criticism of the Roman clergy for usurping the temporal power of princes. The most cursory examination of his teaching concerning the functions of Church and State will suffice to make it clear that our Reformer gave no countenance to theocracy envisaged in this manner.

There can be no doubt that from 1536 to 1541 Geneva was governed by a regime in which the State claimed to direct both the religious and the civil

---

6   Sidney Z. Ehler and John. B. Morrall, *Church and State through the Centuries: a collection of historic documents with commentaries* (London, 1945), 169f. See also *Calvin and Calvinism, Sources of Democracy?*, xiii, 63f.

life of the citizens. This system of caesaropapism prevailed at that period in most of the Swiss towns. Calvin himself was exiled from Geneva because his theological opinions did not meet with the approval of the magistrates.

From 1541 onwards the public life of Geneva was characterized by a conflict which Calvin was compelled to sustain against the magistrates in order to induce them to concede a certain measure of independence to the Church, but even at this period one cannot truly speak of a "theocracy" at Geneva. The popular error is due to confusion between an actual power of Church over State which never existed, and the extraordinary but purely moral ascendancy which Calvin ultimately exercised over the Genevan magistracy towards the close of his life. But it is only from 1555 onwards, that is to say, about nine years before our Reformer's death, that one can speak of an actual ascendancy of Calvin over the magistrates. In any case, it is certain that this purely spiritual ascendancy never constituted authority in the juridical sense of the term.[7]

Cheneviere could have added that Calvin was not even a citizen of the city he supposedly "tyrannized" until 1559—only five years prior to his death.[8]

Another renowned Calvin scholar provides further insight into the confusion of the "Calvin legend" as to Calvin's political views. John T. McNeill writes,

The habitual reference by Calvin to the divine basis of government gives color to the use of such terms

---

7   Marc Chenevier, "Did Calvin Advocate Theocracy," *Evangelical Quarterly*, IX (1937), 160, 168. *Caesaropapism* is, literally, "Caesar is pope-ism." In other words, it the political system in which the state assumes sovereignty over the church, even to the point of appointing its leaders. It is similar to the system known as Erastianism.

8   Kingdon and Linder, *Calvin and Calvinism*, 35.

as "theocracy," "bibliocracy," "christocracy" by some writers who describe his ideal of a political society as the disciplined community of Geneva under his sway. That such terms have been proposed as keys to his political intention is itself significant. But they are not free from ambiguity and are not very helpful toward an understanding of his mind or his Geneva. If "theocracy" is taken in its popular sense of hierocracy, government by priests, rather than in its basic meaning, government by God, it is an inappropriate way to describe the situation at Geneva, for there Calvin separates the magistrate from the clergy. He and his ministerial associates held no political offices or magisterial authority in Geneva. If "bibliocracy" means a government based on biblical principles, it is vaguely applicable; but not if it implies a basis of biblical legislation. The notion that a modern state must not be "ruled by the common laws of nations" but in accordance with "the political system of Moses" Calvin explicitly rejects as "seditious, false, and foolish."[9]

I have thus far briefly stated and refuted the hierocratic interpretation of Calvin. Now the main concern of this chapter, his relation to the social contract theory, democracy, and the theory of just revolution associated with them, must now be taken up. Far more can be said in favor of the theory that Calvin is the father of American democracy, thus the difficulty of this theory warrants investigation far more than the superficialities of the one just refuted. In the course of this chapter, it will become clear that the teaching of Calvin himself in a certain sense contributes to the relatively more difficult character of the issue now taken up.

The thesis of this paper is that Calvin rejected the distinctive tenets of a social contract theory of the origin of civil government and thus the view of democracy and just revolution built on that

---

9   Kingdon and Linder, 72.

theory. Democracy need not imply the social contract theory, nor does the social contract theory necessarily imply democracy. But the popular, modern, and American understanding of democracy weds the two ideas.

In the course of expounding this thesis, three main points will be noticed:

1. Calvin's rejection of the distinctive tenets of the social contract theory (especially as exemplified in his rejection of the theory of just revolution)

2. Calvin's reception of certain tenets often associated with the social contract theory and modern democracy

3. Calvinism's adoption of the distinctive tenets of the social contract theory

Before beginning the course marked out above, a final preliminary remark is necessary. It concerns the meaning of the phrase used above, the *social contract theory*. By this phrase the political theory is designated that asserts all political power is derived from the consent of the governed conferred (at least theoretically) by an original social contract or agreement. This contract results in mutual obligations for both the governed and the governor. The point of importance for our purposes is that the continuance in office of the governor is conditioned on his proper performance of his obligations. If the governor fails in these fundamental obligations, then the dictum becomes operative that what the people give, the people can take away. It must be underscored that this theory as understood in this treatment does not merely assert that government should originate by a social contract but that all government does, in fact, assume such a social contract and depends for its legitimacy as government on the proper fulfillment of the obligations involved in that social contract. In all of this, two points are of central importance for our purposes. First, all governmental power is derived from the people. Second, this implies the right of revolution or forceful resistance to government. What the people give, the people can take away!

II. CALVIN'S REJECTION OF THE DISTINCTIVE TENETS OF THE SOCIAL CONTRACT THEORY

A. *The Evidence for this Rejection Presented*

It is necessary to begin this presentation of Calvin's rejection of the social contract theory by underscoring that it is not anachronistic to speak in this way. It is, at least, only a verbal anachronism. Theories that for our purposes have substantial similarities to the classic statement of the social contract theory by Locke in the seventeenth century were well-known in Calvin's era. Many scholars remark on this fact.[10] This tradition favorable to popular revolution and even tyrannicide can be traced to the later scholastics and through them to Roman law and Greek philosophy.[11] It was a tradition Calvin self-consciously and explicitly rejected. Mueller remarks,

> It is well-known that in the Middle Ages this *mutua obligatio* was conceived in terms of a contractual relation between king and subject. . . . Subsequently, the representatives of natural law taught that the juridical ground of all rule lay in a voluntary and contractual subjection of all the members of the realm. Since the eleventh century these political theorists and later the *Monarchomachi* also taught that the one party of the contract was obligated to the other only to the extent that the other performed its duty. Here Calvin breaks with the tradition which would allow a reservation in case of the default of a

---

10   Kingdon and Linder, 51. W. A. Mueller, *Church and State in Luther and Calvin* (Nashville: Broadman,1954), 153. Quentin Skinner, *The Foundations of Modern Political Thought* (Cambridge: Cambridge University Press, 1978), 2:321f. Waskey, "John Calvin's Theory of Political Obligation," 224.

11   Skinner, *The Foundations of Modern Political Thought*, 2:32f.; Waskey, "John Calvin's Theory of Political Obligation," 24.

ruler. For we have seen that even bad rulers are to be obeyed, provided they do not coerce us to do things that are clearly contrary to God's will.[12]

Other theories justifying revolt were in the air. Lutheran jurists and theologians had appealed to scholastic theories of natural law to justify a private law theory with radical, anarchistic implications.[13]

All this lends greater weight to the evidence that will shortly be cited from Calvin. In asking what Calvin thought of the social contract theory, we are not raising an issue Calvin did not himself confront. Calvin self-consciously rejected such a view. The evidence will show that there is both self-conscious and explicit confrontation with this view and self-conscious and explicit rejection of it.

In examining Calvin's political commitments, scholars have followed a less direct method of discerning Calvin's position by evaluating his influence on governing bodies.[14] Waskey notes that Calvin's juridical influence as one appointed to a commission to codify Geneva's civil laws was not in the democratic direction. "The changes eventually adopted made the city government more orderly but a little less democratic when the right of initiative was transferred from the General Assembly to the Little Council."[15] Others have tried to discern Calvin's political commitments by an analysis of the church government he favored. This procedure is problematic as Calvin made some rather clear distinctions between civil and ecclesiastical government.[16] Georges de Lagarde has argued that the church Calvin established in Geneva was less democratic than the civil government already in place when he came to Geneva.[17] In a much more extensive study, Robert M. Kingdon has argued that Calvin's followers, Beza specifically,

---

12   Mueller, *Church and State in Luther and Calvin*, 153.
13   Skinner, *The Foundations of Modern Political Thought*, 196f.
14   Kingdon and Linder, eds., *Calvin and Calvinism*, 8.
15   Waskey, "John Calvin's Theory of Political Obligation," 21.
16   Waskey, 206, 281, 302. See also Calvin's Commentary on Acts 23:5.
17   Kingdon and Linder, eds., *Calvin and Calvinism*, 8.

feared democracy. This is shown, he thinks, by Beza's advocacy of a centralizing and authoritarian "presbyterianism" as the proper form of government for the French Reform movement as opposed to the decentralizing and democratic congregationalism of Morely.[18]

Of whatever importance all this may be, it certainly is secondary compared to the direct statements of Calvin. We will examine these statements under three headings: the *Institutes*, the Commentaries, and the Letters. It will be shown that, in every possible way, Calvin rejected the substance and consequences of the social contract theory of government and that the pressures of the French situation, which for many became a call to revolution, only served to manifest the depth of his commitment to the theology stated in his other writings.

1. The Institutes

One must begin by noting that the conception that legitimate political power is derived from the people is absent from the *Institutes*. Further, there is no support for the later Calvinist contention that while all political power is ultimately from God, it is mediately from the people.[19] Calvin's tendency to treat all human authority as of the same kind and thus equate fathers and princes is certainly not hospitable to social contract theorists.[20] For Calvin, civil authority is from God—period. This assertion is reinforced by Calvin's insistence that the form of government is irrelevant to the legitimacy of government. When Calvin is about to discuss the relative merits of monarchy, aristocracy, and democracy, he begins with this caution: "Moreover, though there are various forms of magistracy, yet there is no difference in this respect, but we ought to receive them all as ordinances of God" (4:20:7). The whole tone of Calvin's discussion of the various forms of government is one

---

18   Kingdon and Linder, 45f.; R. M. Kingdon, *Geneva and the French Protestant Movement*, 1564–1572, ch. 3.

19   John Legg, "The Christian and Revolution," *Banner of Truth*, CCXLVII (1984), 12. See also *Institutes* 2:8:35, 38; 4:20:22.

20   See *Institutes* 2:8:35, 38.

that makes clear its relative unimportance. He says, "And for private men, who have no authority to deliberate on the regulation of any public affairs, it would surely be a vain occupation to dispute which would be the best form of government in the place where they live" (4:20:8). One who believes in popular sovereignty could never have uttered such a sentiment. Having expressed a preference for aristocracy mixed perhaps with elements of democracy, Calvin is concerned that no one mistake the nature of his preference. Governmental legitimacy is not tied to any specific form of magistracy. "But if those, to whom the will of God has assigned another form of government, transfer this to themselves, so as to be tempted to desire a revolution, the very thought will be not only foolish and useless, but altogether criminal" (4:20:8). This is an explicit rebuke of the social contract theory. We will return to parallel statements in a moment.

Not only does the form of government have no effect on its legitimacy but its moral character also is irrelevant at this point. Calvin states this in 2:8:36 when dealing with the fifth commandment, which he applies to all human authority. "Nor does it make any difference, whether they are worthy of this honor, or not. For whatever be their characters, yet it is not without the appointment of divine providence, that they have attained that station on account of which the supreme legislator has commanded them to be honored." In an extended passage in the concluding chapter of the *Institutes* (4:20:24–29) Calvin makes the same point. Mentioning that thus far he has been speaking only of "a magistrate who truly answers to his title" (4:20:24), he turns his attention to evil magistrates and gives a lurid description of a magistrate in whom there is "no appearance of the image of God." What is the duty of a citizen to such a magistrate? Calvin answers in 4:20:25:

> But, if we direct our attention to the word of God,
> it will carry us much further; even to submit to the
> government, not only of those princes who discharge
> their duty to us with becoming integrity and fidelity,

but of all who possess sovereignty, even though they perform none of the duties of their function. . . . But let us rather insist on the proof of that which the minds of men do not easily admit; that a man of the worst character, and most undeserving of all honor, who holds the sovereign power, really possesses that eminent and Divine authority, which the Lord has given by his word to the ministers of his justice and judgement; and, therefore, that he ought to be regarded by his subjects, as far as pertains public obedience, with the same reverence and esteem which they would show to the best of kings, if such a one were granted to them.

The next three paragraphs of the *Institutes* would provide material to multiply such quotations, but the clarity of Calvin's position makes that unnecessary.

Calvin concludes the paper of the *Institutes* under discussion with several statements that can only be called explicit renunciations of the whole theory of government contained in the sentence: what the people give, they may take away. Calvin rather believes that what God gives, only God can take away. "But it will be said that rulers owe mutual duties to their subjects. That I have already confessed. But he who infers from this that obedience ought to be rendered to none but just rulers, is a very bad reasoner" (4:20:29). Can we do nothing about a tyrannical ruler? Calvin replies, "Nothing remains for us, but to implore the aid of the Lord" (4:20:29). This Calvin is abundantly clear on. It is not our business to correct the injustices of tyrannical government. "For though the correction of tyrannical domination is the vengeance of God, we are not, therefore, to conclude that it is committed to us, who have received no other command than to obey and suffer" (4:20:31). Calvin's distaste for anything like the social contract could not be clearer!

2. The Commentaries

An extensive treatment under this heading is not necessary for the purposes of this chapter. The following remarks will suffice. At several points Calvin makes clear that the worst political evil is anarchy, to which even the worst tyranny is preferable (see also his comments on Acts 23:5; Rom 13:3, and 1 Pet 2:14). This seems to show that in any supposed dialectic between order and freedom, Calvin definitely would come down on the side of order. Calvin also makes clear his rejection of the idea that we may take it upon ourselves to call princes to account (see also his comments on 1 Pet 2:13, 14, 17; Matt 22:21, and Acts 23:5). Calvin's remarks on Acts 23:5 provide unusual insight into the character of his political thought at this point and several others. Thus, we quote them in part:

> Therefore all dignity, which is appointed for maintenance of civil government, ought to be reverenced and had in honour. For whosoever he be that rebelleth against or resisteth the magistrate or those who are appointed to rule and are promoted unto honor he would have no government. And such desire tendeth to the disturbing of order. Yea, it shaketh and overthroweth all humanity. . . . But here riseth a question, whether we ought not to obey a ruler, though he exercise tyranny? For if that man be not to be deprived of honour which executeth his office amiss, Paul offended in robbing the high priest of his honour. Therefore, I answer, that there is some difference between civil magistrates and the prelates of the church. For though the exploiting administration of earthly or civil rule be confused or perverse, yet the Lord will have men to continue in subjection. But when the spiritual government doth degenerate, the consciences of the godly are at liberty.

There is, however, one point at which the commentaries may clarify a point Calvin does not touch on in the *Institutes*. Calvin has demonstrated that the legitimacy of government is tied neither to its form nor its moral character. One loophole remains that the commentaries close. For now, Calvin asserts that the legitimacy of government is not tied to its origin. Commenting on Romans 13:1, Calvin asserts,

> It seems indeed to me, that the Apostle intended by this word to take away the frivolous curiosity of men, who are wont often to inquire by what right they who rule have obtained their authority; but it ought to be enough for us, that they do rule; for they have not ascended by their own power into this high station, but they have been placed there by the Lord's hand.

Calvin's comments on 1 Peter 2:13–14 also emphasize this point:

> As Peter referred especially to the Roman Emperor, it was necessary to add this admonition; for it is certain that the Romans through unjust means rather than in a legitimate way penetrated into Asia and subdued these countries. Besides, the Caesars, who then reigned, had possessed themselves of the monarchy by tyrannical force. Hence Peter as it were forbids these things to be controverted, for he shews that subjects ought to obey their rulers without hesitation because they are not made eminent, unless elevated by God's hand.

It may be necessary to underscore that in such passages Calvin is thinking exclusively of those who possess actual civil power when he speaks of submitting to civil authorities who gained that power by tyrannical force *in the past* but now are the recognized civil authorities. He is not speaking of those who through unjust means are *now in the present* attempting to overthrow the civil authorities and usurp the civil powers of a land. Calvin clearly would have opposed such revolutionaries.

3. The Letters (especially regarding the French Reform Movement)
Calvin's passionate solicitude for the French Reform movement
is no secret to any student of Calvin's life and ministry. France
was his native country. The vindication of the French Reform
movement from the charge of Anabaptism was the originating
motive for the *Institutes*. The progress of the French Reform is the
dominating interest of the letters of the last five years of his life. It
alternately fills him with joy and breaks his heart and calls forth
his most earnest counsel and entreaty. Indeed, it is perhaps not too
much to say that it is the central burden of his life.

What, then, will Calvin's response be to the growing pressure
on and in this movement to revolt against the "powers that be"?
Here, if anywhere in Calvin, we shall explore the depths of Calvin's
soul on political matters. What will Calvin's response be to the
revolutionary pressures generated by the bitter persecution of his
beloved French Reform movement?

The answer to this question is not difficult to discover. Calvin's
reaction to the least smell of political insurrection fills his letters
to the French Reform from the first to the last. It is intimated as
early as 1553 in his letter to the five condemned prisoners at Lyon.
"While it pleases God to give his enemies the rein, our duty is to
be quiet, although the time of our redemption tarries."[21]

In 1557 he writes to the church at Paris, now a large body with
a growing number of members from a higher stratum of society:

> But whatever view we take of the case, our true wisdom
> is to submit ourselves to him, and, though everything
> be perplexed, to wait peaceably and in silence for
> the deliverance which he has promised. In the mean
> time, my dear brethren, we pray you to practice the
> lesson that has been taught us by the great Master, to
> possess our souls in patience. We know how difficult
> that is for the flesh, but recollect also that then is the

---

21   John Calvin, *Calvin's Selected Works*, ed. by Jules Bonnet and trans. by David
Constable (Grand Rapids, 1983), 5:407.

moment to strive against ourselves and our passions, when we are assailed by our enemies. And esteem it not to be weak defence. . . . Let it be your study to attempt nothing which is not warranted by his word. . . . . If we go beyond the limits he has prescribed to us, let us always fear to receive at last the wages of our temerity. We say not this as being bold at your expense, but because we are well aware that in such terrors one may be urged to many undertakings in which it is difficult to preserve moderation....And indeed better it were that we were all involved in ruin, than that the gospel of God should be exposed to the reproach of arming men to sedition and tumult; for God will always cause the ashes of his servants to fructify, but excesses and violence will bring with them nothing but barrenness.[22]

Calvin's counsel steadfastly continued in the same vein as the persecution worsened. He counseled against any public demonstration, against the seizing of temples in strongly Protestant areas.[23] He is disgusted by a minister who led such an armed insurrection.[24] He even argues against resisting a "mutinous populace" not led by civil magistrates and declares he would punish Protestant outbreaks of these kinds in the same way the king was punishing them.[25] Calvin's response to the smashing of idols by a Protestant mob in a Roman Catholic temple exhibits his position clearly:

We speak of the foolish deed which was performed at Sauve in burning idols and pulling down a cross. We are very much surprised at such temerity in a man whose duty it was to moderate and restrain others. . . . God has never given commandment, except to

---

22 Calvin, 6:360, 361.
23 Calvin, 7:92, 95, 98, 173, 182, 190.
24 Calvin, 7:269–271.
25 Calvin, 7:238.

> each one in his own house, and in public to those he
> arms with authority, to cast down idols. . . . But since
> obedience is better than sacrifice, we have to consider
> what is lawful, and restrain ourselves within bounds.
> For it is to act like a horse that has broke loose from
> the reins to attempt more than what our vocation
> warrants."[26]

This, of course, is not the only element in Calvin's political
counsels to the French Brethren. As shall be seen a bit later in
this chapter, Calvin, while rejecting all violent resistance to civil
authority by private citizens, did believe both that on some
occasions there might be legitimate doubt as to whom our civil
authorities are and that the proper civil authorities had the duty to
forcefully resist the injustice of tyrannizing civil authorities. Quite
consistently then, when princes of the blood royal, namely the king
of Navarre and the prince of Conde, adopted the Protestant cause,
he was ready to urge them to constitutional activity in protection
of the Huguenots. This was, of course, consistent with Calvin's
conviction that the chief duty of the magistrate was to uphold
the true religion.[27] Calvin, then, is deeply involved in energetically
calling such civil magistrates to action and in guiding their actions
by very detailed plans and counsels.[28] In all this, however, Calvin
never departs from his anti-revolutionary principles. In the very
letter addressed to Beza, his emissary to the king of Navarre,
in which his intention to stir the king to action is made clear,
he also goes on record as opposed to the unwarrantable warlike
demonstrations of certain Protestants.[29]

In a letter to Bullinger, he can speak in the same sentence of
Beza's stimulating the king's sluggishness and counteracting the
turbulent counsels of many.[30] What most clearly underscores this

---

26   Calvin, 7:205, 206.
27   Calvin, 6:245, 246; 7:290–293. See also 4:20:3, 9 of the *Institutes*.
28   Calvin 7:126, 138, 145, 161, 223f.
29   Calvin, 7:129.
30   Calvin, 7:138.

point is Calvin's counsel to the Huguenot soldiery after the foolish peace concluded by the Prince of Conde in early 1563. Though Calvin despised the vanity and folly of this peace, the duty of the Huguenot warriors is clear:

> You have now to practice the doctrine of the Holy Scriptures which is that if God takes away the sword from those he had girt with it, this change should make us give way and regulate our conduct accordingly. Wherefore, I do not see that you have any reason or power, approved by God, to resist a council of which it is impossible to say now that it is not legitimate. I cannot dissemble that everybody is displeased with the prince for showing himself so accommodating, and still more so for being in such a hurry to conclude. It seems pretty evident also that he has provided better for his own personal safety than for the common repose of the poor brethren. But be that as it will, this single consideration ought to shut our mouths, that we know that it is the will of God again to exercise us. I shall always give my advice to abstain from arms, and that all of us should perish rather than have recourse, a second time to the disorders which we have witnessed.[31]

Also of interest in Calvin's letters, though not on the subject of France but rather of England, is Calvin's distancing himself from Knox's blast against women in civil authority, in which Knox argued that the government of such women is illegitimate. Calvin may have had several objections to Knox's willingness to tie the legitimacy of government to the moral character of that government:

> Finally I added in conclusion, that since by custom, common consent, and long established usage, it had been admitted that kingdoms and principalities might be by hereditary right transmitted to women, it did not seem proper to me that this question

---

31   Calvin, 7:295f., 302.

> should be mooted, not only because the thing was
> odious in itself, but because in my judgement it is not
> permitted to unsettle governments that have been set
> up by the peculiar providence of God.[32]

The Conspiracy of Amboise provides perhaps the clearest evidence of the extent of Calvin's dislike of any revolutionary activity whatever. The secrecy of such political plots complicates the account scholars give of the details of this incident. Consequently, it is much discussed.[33] Kingdon thinks that Beza encouraged the plot.[34] However this may be, Calvin's letters present a very consistent picture of his attitude toward the whole matter. Unless we are willing to accuse Calvin of deliberate and continued duplicity and falsehood, we must conclude from his letters that his attitude toward it was from the beginning severely negative. Writing to Sturm on March 23, 1560, three days after the abortive failure of the conspiracy and before he knew its outcome, Calvin says,

> When I was at first consulted by those who were the
> prime instigators in this business, I frankly replied
> that their whole manner of proceeding displeased me,
> but that the transaction itself was what incurred my
> greatest disapprobation, because what they foolishly
> resolved they next set about childishly.[35]

It is true that, in a very qualified form, their action would have been given Calvin's approval, though it must be quickly added that the plot as it actually took place in no sense had his approval. In a letter to Peter Martyr on May 11, 1560, Calvin mentions he would have approved of the prince of Conde presenting to the king a confession, but only on the condition that "they should be

---

32   Calvin, 7:47.
33   N. M. Sutherland, *The Huguenot Struggle for Recognition* (New Haven, 1980).
34   R. M. Kingdon, "The Political Resistance of the Calvinists if France and the Low Countries," *Church History*, XXVII (1985), 224.
35   Calvin, 7:91.

perfectly on their guard not to shed blood" if they had to defend the Prince.[36] In his more extended defense addressed to Admiral Coligny, he says,

> I admitted, it is true, that if the princes of the blood demanded to be maintained in their rights for the common good, and if the Parliament joined them in their quarrel, that it would then be lawful for all good subjects to lend them armed assistance. The man afterwards asked me, if one of the princes of the blood, though not the first in rank, had decided upon taking such a step, were we not then warranted to support him? I again gave him an answer in the negative with regard to this supposition.[37]

Statements like these make clear the extent to which Calvin was willing to maintain his anti-revolutionary principles. Had there been the least pragmatism in Calvin's attitude, he surely could have found a way to justify a rebellion led by one of the princes of blood. Sutherland's comment seems correct: "The explanation of the tenacity with which he pursued this purpose and declined to support any other [the reference is to the King of Navarre's armed protection of the rights and liberties of the Huguenots] lies in his political philosophy. To Calvin, it was only through the agency of Navarre and his legitimate claim to power that any alteration of the government in France could be undertaken."[38]

The claim could be made that Calvin's objections to the conspiracy of Amboise were prudential rather than doctrinal in character. In other words, it could be argued that Calvin did not object to it because of anti-revolutionary principles but because he feared its practical results. No dichotomy should be drawn between these alternatives. Both considerations, the prudential

---

36   Calvin, 7:107.

37   Calvin, 7:176f.

38   J. H. M. Salmon, ed., *The French Wars of Religion, How Important were the Religious Factors?* (Boston, 1967), 16f. The reference is to the king of Navarre's armed protection of the rights and liberties of the Huguenots.

and the doctrinal, led to his opposition, but it is likely he feared for the results precisely because the conspiracy seemed to violate the principles of the Word of God. The following statement of Calvin from his defense of his actions in the matter in his letter to Admiral Coligny corroborates the statements made above:

> However I have never dissembled my opinion about that transaction, when I was questioned respecting it, as on the present occasion I am quite disposed, if you wish, Monseigneur, to hear a brief abstract of it, to lay before you the whole truth. Seven or eight months before the event, a certain person entrusted with the command of some troops consulted me, whether it was not lawful to resist the tyranny by which the children of God were then oppressed, and what means might be employed for that purpose. As I perceived that opinions of this sort were becoming generally current, after having given him a peremptory answer that he should abandon all thoughts of this kind, I strove to demonstrate to him that he had no warrant for such conduct according to God; and that even according to the world such measures were ill-concerted, presumptuous, and could have no successful issue.[39]

The phrases "according to God" and "according to the world" clearly indicate that Calvin was self-consciously opposing the Amboise conspiracy for both doctrinal and prudential reasons.

The conclusion is necessary that Calvin resolutely continued in the full practice of non-revolutionary principles even in the face of the rising revolutionary tendencies of the Huguenot movement. "But to me it is enough that God approves of my diligence, and even more than enough to have in my favour the testimony of impartial and moderate men: these are not in a majority it is true, but I prefer their calm judgments to the noisy outcries of the multitude."[40]

---

39 Calvin, 7:176f.
40 Calvin, 7:153.

B. *The Supposed Evidence to the Contrary Treated*

Notwithstanding the massive and clear evidence already surveyed, scholars have sought the source of later Calvinistic revolutionary theories in Calvin himself.[41] Hudson asserts,

> The major current of Calvinism, beginning with Ponet, Goodman, Hotman, Mornay, and other contemporaries of Calvin, solved this problem in the same way in which many earlier political theorists had solved it. They assumed that God delegated his powers to the people before delegating them to the magistrates, and that, therefore, the people were in a position superior to that of the magistrate. Although the power was derived from God, the people were given the determining voice as to the manner in which the power should be exercised—that is to say, ultimate sovereignty may reside in God but it is mediated through the people. The actual powers of government, qualified, to be sure, by divine requirements, rest upon the consent of the governed. This type of thinking would have been congenial to the mature Calvin.[42]

As the phrase "mature Calvin" suggests, such a theory of Calvin's political thought is often associated with the idea there is a discernible drift in Calvin, especially in his later years, toward the social contract theory and democracy.[43] These words from Hudson cite evidence that show that an element of truth, at least, must be recognized here.

> Calvin's convictions as to what constituted the most desirable form of government underwent progressive change during the years. In the first edition of the *Institutes* before his arrival in Geneva, aristocracy had

---

41 *Calvin and Calvinism*, 3. *The French Wars*, 10f. Skinner, 192, 220.
42 *Calvin and Calvinism*, 23.
43 Skinner, *The Foundations of Modern Political Thought*.

his preference. After seven years' experience in the Swiss city, he favored "either aristocracy or a mixture of aristocracy and democracy" such as was practiced in Geneva.[44]

As has been seen, however, Calvin never connected the legitimacy of government to its form.

Another tendency of those who adopt this view of Calvin is to see Calvin's political viewpoints as self-contradictory. Hudson says, "Calvin's counsel of unlimited and unqualified obedience is rather deceptive and provides G.P. Gooch with the basis for his charge that Calvin indulged in political double-talk."[45] By itself, this tendency raises questions about the theory under discussion. Leaving aside one's personal conviction that Calvin was among the most consistent of theologians, any theory that is forced to the expedient of claiming that Calvin contradicted himself, thereby manifests the possibility it has misunderstood Calvin.

The evidence already cited creates the greatest presumption against the theory under discussion. It is only necessary to present specific alternatives to the interpretations by which it purports to support itself. Five such interpretations and arguments will now be taken up.

1. *"Calvin suggested that there were magistrates of the people who had for their duty leading revolts in the event of tyranny."*

The famous sentences to which this argument has reference are found in the *Institutes* (4:20:31):

> For though the correction of tyrannical domination is the vengeance of God, we are not, therefore, to conclude that it is committed to us, who have received no other command than to obey and suffer. This observation I always apply to private persons. For if

---

44   *Calvin and Calvinism,* 17, 22.
45   *Calvin and Calvinism,* 20; Skinner, *The Foundations of Modern Political Thought,* 192, 214.

there be, in the present day, any magistrates appointed for the protection of the people and the moderation of the power of kings, such as were, in ancient times, the Ephori, who were a check upon the kings among the Lacedaemonians, or the popular tribunes upon the consuls among the Athenians; or with power such as perhaps is now possessed by the three estates in every kingdom when they are assembled; I am so far from prohibiting them, in the discharge of their duty, to oppose the violence or cruelty of kings, that I affirm, that if they connive at kings in their oppression of their people, such forbearance involves the most nefarious perfidy, because they fraudulently betray the liberty of the people, of which they know that they have been appointed protectors by the ordination of God.

It is tempting to view this statement as a lone and undeveloped concession to the popular distaste for tyranny and especially the persecution of Protestants. There are important senses in which this would be true. Certainly, the lack of biblical citation and the presence of heathen examples ought to be a caution to us in using this statement to overthrow the massive biblical structure of Calvin's political thought. Nonetheless, evidence exists that this statement is neither lone nor undeveloped in Calvin's writings. In 4:20:23 of the *Institutes*, Calvin is careful to note that when he says private citizens should not take government business into their own hands, he does not mean they may not bear arms under the command of the civil magistrate. Many constructions could be put upon these words, but they are certainly appropriate ones to remember if and when a "magistrate of the people" should have to resist tyranny. Waskey asserts that no trace of this, Calvin's theory of resistance to tyranny, can be found in his New Testament commentaries.[46] This is certainly significant. There may, however, be an implicit allusion to it in the comments of Calvin on Romans

---

46   Waskey, 249.

13:1: "He calls them *higher powers*, not the supreme, who possess the chief authority, but such as excel other men. Magistrates are then thus called with regard to their subjects and not as compared with each other." Is this an innocent exegetical remark? Perhaps, but it is very easy to see a side reference to Calvin's "magistrates of the people." Skinner cites Calvin's *Homilies on I Samuel*, Sermon 29. This reference does, indeed, restate the theory of 4:20:31 of the *Institutes* quite completely.[47] Whatever one thinks of Calvin's true meaning at this point, one must acknowledge that the famous sentences cited above formed the point of contact for the development of the later Calvinistic theories of revolution from Calvin.[48]

Several remarks, some quite obvious, may be made that totally disassociate Calvin from the later Calvinistic revolutionary theories:

a. Scholars like to denominate the theory of Calvin under discussion his theory of revolution. It is not mere logomachy to complain about such terminology. Armed resistance by civil authorities constitutionally appointed for the specific purpose of resisting tyranny can scarcely be called revolution in any proper sense of the word. One fails to see how such a theory could ever be thought to contradict in any sense his other anti-revolutionary statements. To obey such rulers and assist such magistrates in their armed resistance to tyranny would be the purest submission to civil authority.

b. Calvin's statement is clearly tentative, cautious, and conditional. "If there be . . . magistrates appointed for the protection of the people . . . or with power such as perhaps is now possessed by the three estates." Calvin does not assert that to be legitimate, a government must include such magistrates. Elsewhere he clearly asserts the

---

47 Skinner, *The Foundations of Modern Political Thought*, 214.
48 *Calvin and Calvinism*, 21, 36.

opposite. He does not assert any such magistrates do in fact exist in the Europe of his day. All this is in doubt. To remark, as some scholars do, that Calvin knew no pure monarchy really existed in the Europe of his day is to view Calvin as cynical.[49] Calvin's conduct in his counsel to the French Reform exhibits just how unsure he actually was that his "magistrates of the people" existed in France. He certainly opposed any armed resistance except that led by those with the strongest claims to the supreme authority.

c. This introduces our third remark. There is the clearest distinction between what Calvin says and the later Calvinistic position that asserted inferior magistrates had the religious duty to resist tyranny. It is doubtful Calvin's "Ephori" may be equated with the "inferior magistrates" of which later Calvinistic thought spoke. Skinner says, "But it seems misleading to suggest . . . that Calvin's analysis exhibits nothing more than an 'almost literal conformity' with Bucer's theory of inferior magistrates, and that we ought not to think of Calvin's popular magistrates as representatives of the people. . . . Calvin never alludes to the concept of inferior magistrates in this (or any other) discussion about political resistance."[50] Certainly Calvin does not assert that "magistrates of the people" actually existed. He did not act as if they existed in his counsel to the French Reform.

d. Skinner goes on to claim, however, that Calvin's "Ephori" are by Calvin himself thought of as elected officials for that reason responsible to the people. In this way he seeks to explain their duty to armed resistance to tyranny and find a precursor of the later social contract theories of political thought. Lloyd, seconded by Stein and Ullmann, disputes the idea that Calvin is thinking of elected

---

49 *Calvin and Calvinism*, 20, 22.
50 Skinner, *The Foundations of Modern Political Thought*, 232.

officials.[51] Basing his argument on the peculiar Latin phrases Calvin employs in this section, he maintains that the model for Calvin's "magistrates of the people" is not an elected official in a modern social contract system of government but a Roman guardian. He concludes,

> It is inconceivable that Calvin introduced so many juridical allusions inadvertently into his concluding statement. In affirming the duty of magisterial guardians to resist royal arbitrariness, he had no intention of arguing a democratic case. The popular magistrates were not 'elected' by their ward, the people, and they were not 'responsible' to the latter. They were appointed by the only authority competent to do so—namely, God himself.[52]

Lloyd effectively casts doubt on the democratic interpretation of the "Ephori."

1. *"Calvin made government responsible to the people."*

The statement made by Calvin in his comments on Romans 13:1 is frequently cited in proof of a social contract interpretation of Calvin's political thought. He says there, "In short, they [the civil magistrates] are responsible to God and to men in the exercise of their power." One may have to admit that Calvin's language is confusing to us here. We naturally associate such a statement with the social contract view that asserts that if such responsibilities to us are not properly carried out, we may correct the situation, by revolt if necessary. This is, of course, precisely the opposite of what Calvin would say and, in fact, did say:

---

51   H. A. Lloyd, "Calvin and the Duty of Guardians to Resist," *Journal of Ecclesiastical History*, XXXII (1981), 65–67. Peter Stein, "Calvin and the Duty of Guardians to Resist: A Comment," *Journal of Ecclesiastical History*, XXXII (1981), 69–70. Walter Ullmann, "Calvin and the Duty of Guardians to Resist: A Further Comment," *Journal of Ecclesiastical History*, XXXII (1981), 499–501.
52   Lloyd, 67.

> But it will be said, that rulers owe mutual duties to their subjects. That I have already confessed. But he who infers from this that obedience ought to be rendered to none but just rulers, is a very bad reasoner. For husbands owe mutual duties to their wives, and parents to their children. Now, if husbands and parents violate their obligations, . . . does it follow that children should be less obedient to their parents, or wives to their husbands? (*Institutes* 4:20.29)

Lloyd's suggestion noted above that we should find the model for Calvin's "Ephori" in the Roman guardians is also instructive as to what sense we should put upon the phrase "responsible to men."

2. *"Calvin disliked monarchy and felt it was a very bad form of government."*

This is undoubtedly the case, but we have seen that Calvin refused to permit revolution to correct a bad form of government. A word must be said, however, about the classic citation from Calvin that epitomizes his hostility: "It very rarely happens that kings regulate themselves so that their will is never at variance with justice and rectitude." That word we may permit Calvin to speak: "But if those, to whom the will of God has assigned another form of government, transfer this to themselves so as to be tempted to desire a revolution, the very thought will be not only foolish and useless, but altogether criminal." (*Institutes* 4:20:8)

3. *"Calvin used the language of resistance against rulers."*

The words of Calvin frequently cited in relation to this are his comments on Hosea 5:11: "We now see how vain is the excuse of those who say that they ought to obey king; . . . true, when the king commanded nothing contrary to God's word; but when he perverted God's worship, when he set up corrupt superstitions, then the people ought to have firmly resisted him."[53]

53 John Calvin, *Calvin's Commentaries* (Grand Rapids: Baker Book House, 1981), 13:205.

It must first be stated that the term *resisted* is ambiguous, not necessarily implying revolution. Further, both the previous evidence and the context of this particular statement show Calvin is thinking only of disobedience when he in this place uses the word *resist*. Really, Calvin's use of such a word in this way speaks in favor of an anti-revolutionary interpretation. The point is this: For Calvin, so strong was the legitimate authority of princes that for a subject even to disobey required psychologically an act of positive resistance.

4. *"Calvin taught that when civil magistrates command things contrary to God's law, they abrogated their authority."*

This line of argument is perhaps the most plausible of those brought to show a revolutionary drift in Calvin's thinking. Skinner attempts to establish the point:

> The only important exception appears to be Calvin himself. When he published the final Latin edition of his *Institutes* in 1559, he inserted into the final chapter, for the first time, a single dramatic phrase which appears at least to contain an allusion to the private-law theory of resistance. The wording is (as, ever) highly equivocal, and includes no mention of the idea that, if a ruler exceeds his legitimate authority, he automatically reduces himself to the status of a felonious private citizen. But the passage does contain the clear suggestion that a ruler who goes beyond the bounds of his office automatically ceases to count as a genuine magistrate. Calvin points to the example of Daniel, when he "denies that he has committed any offence against the King when he has not obeyed his impious edict" [4:20:32 of the *Institutes*]. The reason this was justified, Calvin is now prepared to claim, is that "the King had exceeded his limits, and had not only done an injury to men, but, by raising his arm against God, had degraded his own authority."[54]

54   Skinner, *The Foundations of Modern Political Thought*, 219f.

McNeill cites the comments on Daniel 6:22. While McNeill himself does not explicitly draw revolutionary conclusions from these comments, the implication may be present in his general presentation.

> Two years after the last Latin edition of the *Institutes*, commenting on Daniel 6:22, "Before thee, O King, I have done no hurt," he [Calvin] observes:

> For earthly princes lay aside their power when they rise up against God, and are unworthy to be reckoned among the number of mankind. We ought rather utterly to defy them [*conspuere in ipsorum capita*, literally, "to spit on their very heads"] than to obey them.[55]

In rounding out the evidence for this interpretation of Calvin, Calvin's comments on Acts 5:29 may be cited:

> God doth set men over us in such sort with power that he keepeth still his own authority safe and sound. Therefore, we must obey rulers so far, that the commandment of God be not broken...Yea, man is nothing else but an instrument of God....But so soon as rulers do lead us away from the obedience of God, because they strive against God with sacrilegious boldness, their pride must be abated, that God may be above all in authority. Then all smokes of honour vanish away. For God doth not vouchsafe to bestow honourable titles upon men, to the end they may darken his glory. Therefore, if a father, being not content with his own estate, do essay to take from God the chief honour of a father, he is nothing else but a man. If a king, or ruler, or magistrate, do become so lofty that he diminisheth the honour and authority of God, he is but a man. We must thus think also of pastors.

---

55   *Calvin and Calvinism*, 65.

If the plausible interpretation of these passages now being considered were correct, Calvin would be teaching the social contract view of civil government very clearly. The thesis would then have to be that Calvin utterly contradicted himself or that he reversed his thought at a crucial point during the closing periods of his life. This latter view would gain some credit from the fact that the dates of the works of Calvin cited above are 1559, 1561, and 1560, respectively. The following considerations, however, show the fallacy of such a theory.

- The rather startlingly defiant language of Calvin on Daniel 6:22, especially as literally translated by McNeill, seems to run counter to Calvin's repeated inculcation of the duty of honoring all civil authority, even tyrants. An examination of the original context of the statement and particularly a close examination of the statement itself relieves this difficulty. For Calvin does not say that we ought to spit on the heads of our civil authorities. He does not say this even if we understand his words literally. What he actually says is that if it were a question of the most appropriate behavior in response to an edict of a king that required disobedience to God, then, Calvin says, it would be more appropriate to spit on their heads than to allow them to, so to speak, wrest God from his throne by thinking they can in that kind of a situation command our obedience. Calvin's words are rhetorical, a comparison of two extremes, and not to be taken as (even a figurative) command.

- The words of Calvin cited from the *Institutes* are parallel with those from his commentary on Acts in that both appear to teach that human authority ceases in every respect to be authority when it commands contrary to God's law. To this the words of Calvin on Daniel 6:22 are parallel when he speaks of earthly princes laying aside their power.

2. It would be perfectly legitimate merely to assert that all Calvin is thinking of in these passages is that for the purposes

of obedience in any specific situation where God's law is contravened, we ought to look at a civil magistrate as a mere man. In light of the evidence already cited in this book, such an interpretation would be very credible. There are, however, clear reasons internal to these passages to adopt this interpretation.

3. We must, first of all, appreciate that Calvin's theory of human authority is one in which God never diminishes his own authority. The only authority civil magistrates possess is that of being God's representative. The only reason they are to be obeyed is because they are, so to speak, God to us. When, however, they contravene God's will, the individual magistrate "is nothing else but a man."

4. This understanding of Calvin is abundantly supported by his treatment of civil authority in his exposition of the moral law and especially the fifth commandment in the *Institutes*. For Calvin, the command to honor our parents includes by extension the duty of honoring all those God places over us. Thus, in this treatment as in his comments on Acts 5, he lumps together parents, magistrates, and pastors. Note this in his theory of their authority as given in 2:8:35:

> For to those, to whom he gives any preeminence, he communicates his own authority, as far as is necessary for the preservation of that preeminence. The titles of Father, God, and Lord are so eminently applicable to him, that, whenever we hear either of them mentioned, our minds cannot but be strongly affected with a sense of his majesty. Those, therefore, on whom he bestows these titles, he illuminates with a ray of his splendour, to render them all honourable in their respective stations. Thus in a father we ought to recognize something Divine; for it is not without reason that he bears one of the titles of the Deity.

Our prince, or our Lord, enjoys an honour somewhat
similar to that which is given to God.

With this theory of their power, Calvin's words
regarding the necessity of disobedience become clear.
Note how parallel the language of the *Institutes* is to the
passages from Calvin cited in support of the theory under
consideration:

Wherefore the submission exercised towards
them ought to be a step towards honouring the
Supreme Father. Therefore, if they instigate us to
any transgression of the law, we may justly consider
them not as parents, but as strangers, who attempt
to seduce us from obedience to our real Father. The
same observation is applicable to princes, lords, and
superiors of every description. For it is infamous and
absurd, that their eminence should avail to depreciate
the preeminence of God, upon which it depends, and
to which it ought to conduct us. (2:8:38)

Two things impressively call into question and in
fact totally refute a social contract interpretation of such
language. The first is its place in the *Institutes* alongside
Calvin's emphatic anti-revolutionary statements. Yet even
more important is the fact that Calvin includes parents
as well as civil magistrates as among those who cease to
count as authority for us when they command us contrary
to God's law. Can Calvin mean that our duty in every sense
ceases to them when once they contravene God's law? Can
he mean that in no sense of the word they are our parents
and that they are henceforth not to be honored as such?
The very idea is absurd. Why, then, should we entertain
the analogous theory in regard to civil magistrates? There
is no justification for the social contract interpretation of
such language internal to Calvin's thought. Internal to his
thought there is every reason to reject it.

III. CALVIN'S RECEPTION OF CERTAIN TENETS OFTEN ASSOCIATED WITH THE SOCIAL CONTRACT THEORY AND MODERN DEMOCRACY

Calvin stood for limited government and against every form of human absolutism. God alone was sovereign over all. Calvin's political views tended toward the development of human liberty and freedom of thought. This has already been seen, at least in germinal form, in his call for civil disobedience to all commands of government that contravene God's Word and in the theistic theory of human authority that grounded that call.

It is the fact stated above that complicates our assessment of Calvin's relation to modern democracy. Though there is no necessary correlation between democracy and limited government (as Calvin himself would have reminded us—the *Institutes* 4:20:8), in the popular mind, this connection is certainly widespread in our day. Hudson illustrates this with his description of modern democracy.

> In assessing the influence of Calvinism in the development of modern democracy, we must give our attention, first of all, to the twin pillars upon which democracy rest: (1) the idea of limited sovereignty, of a government under law, of limits beyond which government cannot go and to which it must conform; (2) the right of resistance when these limits are exceeded.[56]

If by resistance Hudson means *revolution* (as is probable), then we have seen that Calvin is not a father of democracy in Hudson's sense of the word. The idea of limited sovereignty is, however, a genuine Calvinistic idea.

Besides the evidence already mentioned above for this assertion, there are two aspects of his political thought that clearly corroborate it: his view of the relation of church and state and his view of the ideal form of civil government.

---

56 *Calvin and Calvinism*, 18.

A. Calvin's View of the Relation of Church and State

Calvin stood against both the old church absolutism of the Roman papacy and the rising state absolutism of the European monarchies. In so doing, Calvin took the historic step of separating church and state and limiting the authority of each as over against the other. He thus coordinated them in human society rather than subordinating them one to the other. To put it in the technical, philosophical terminology of Gordon J. Spykman, he taught sphere sovereignty rather than sphere subsidiarity in the mold of medieval Catholicism.[57] The evidence for and exposition of this assertion will be collated under several headings:

1. Calvin against State Absolutism

Kik and Mueller detail Calvin's historic struggle against the Genevan civil authorities for disciplinary control over the Lord's Table.[58] Small as the area of church sovereignty was that Calvin fought for—leaving the council in charge of far too much from our modern viewpoint— the principle at stake was of very large proportions indeed. Spykman's translation of Bavinck's comments is apropos.

> Calvin drew the boundary lines between church and state clearly and sharply, but he drew them differently than we do; the domain within which they had their say was much larger than we would define it today. . . . Nevertheless, the relationship between church and state was contractual and free.[59]

Calvin spoke of this principle in other places. There is an interesting qualification in 4:20:3 of the *Institutes*, where Calvin has been stating his belief that civil authority has the duty of

---

57   David E. Holwerda, ed., *Exploring the Heritage of John Calvin* (Grand Rapids: Baker, 1976).

58   M. K. Kik, *Church and State: The Story of Two Kingdoms* (New York, 1963). See also Mueller, 125f.

59   Holwerda, ed., *Exploring the Heritage of John Calvin*, 202.

upholding the true religion: "For I do not allow men to make laws respecting religion and the worship of God now, any more than I did before."

Calvin's comments on Amos 7:10–13 are perhaps of the greatest interest. In them, Calvin criticizes the state absolutism of both England and Germany:

> And how many are there . . . who accumulate on kings all the authority and power they can, in order that no dispute may be made about religion; but power is to be vested in one king to determine according to his own will whatever he pleases, and this is to remain fixed without any dispute. They who at first extolled Henry, King of England, were certainly inconsiderate men; they gave him the supreme power in all things: and this always vexed me grievously; for they were guilty of blasphemy when they called him the chief Head of the Church under Christ. This was certainly too much. . . . What then is chiefly required of kings is this—to use the sword, with which they are invested, to render free the worship of God. But still they are inconsiderate men, who give them too much power in spiritual things, and this evil is everywhere dominant in Germany; and in these regions it prevails too much.

Thus, every form of state absolutism—whether in Catholic, Anglican, or Lutheran lands—is rejected as making the civil magistrates "too spiritual."[60]

2. Calvin against Church Absolutism

Calvin's hostility to the church absolutism of the Roman papacy ought to be no secret, but it was not mere hostility to the papacy.

---

60   Note the alternate translation of "who give them too much power in spiritual things" in the text of the edition of Calvin's commentaries published Baker Book House, 14:350.

Calvin consistently resisted any tendency to such an absolutism in Geneva. Spykman cites this significant excerpt from Calvin's *Ecclesiastical Ordinances*.

> Let all be done in such a manner as to keep from the ministers any civil jurisdiction whatever, so that they use only the spiritual sword of the Word of God as Paul ordered them, and that thus the Consistory may in no wise derogate from the authority of the magistrates or of civil justice, but rather that the civil power be kept intact.[61]

Having refused to subordinate the civil authorities to the ecclesiastical, it is no surprise that Calvin condemned the Roman Church's claim to immunity from civil prosecution (4:11:15, 16 of the *Institutes*).

Calvin's opposition to church absolutism becomes clear at many points in the *Institutes* (4:11:8, 9, 13). The statement of 4:8:1 epitomizes Calvin's view:

> The power of the church, therefore, is not to be depreciated, yet it must be circumscribed by certain limits, that it may not be extended in every direction, according to the caprice of men. It will, therefore, be highly useful to observe how it is described by the prophets and apostles. For if we simply grant to men the power which they may be pleased to assume, it must be obvious to every one, what a door will be opened for tyranny, which ought never to be seen in the Church of Christ.

The closing words of this quotation show Calvin is interested in the result of the circumscription of church authority, the avoidance of tyranny. Though this is spoken of ecclesiastical tyranny, in such a statement the general tendency of Calvin's opposition to all absolutism becomes clear.

---

61   Holwerda, ed., *Exploring the Heritage of John Calvin*, 200.

3. Calvin for the Separation and Limitation of Church and State

One may deduce from Calvin's limitation of both church and state in the foregoing his separating church and state. There are also clear statements of this in his writings. The classic statement of this is perhaps that given us in 3:19:15 of the *Institutes*:

> To prevent anyone from falling into this error, let us therefore consider, in the first place, that man is under two kinds of government—one spiritual, by which the conscience is formed to piety and the service of God; the other political, by which a man is instructed in the duties of humanity and civility, which are to be observed in an intercourse with mankind. They are generally, and not improperly, denominated the spiritual and the temporal jurisdiction; indicating that the former species of government pertains to the life of the soul, and that the latter relates to the concerns of the present state; not only to the provision of food and clothing, but to the enactment of laws to regulate a man's life among his neighbours by the rules of holiness, integrity, and sobriety. For the former has its seat in the interior of the mind, whilst the latter only directs the external conduct: one may be termed a spiritual kingdom, and the other a political one. But these two, as we have distinguished, always require to be considered separately; and while the one is under discussion, the mind must be abstracted from all consideration of the other. For man contains, as it were, two worlds, capable of being governed by various rulers and various laws.

This long quotation contains many points of significance; specifically, the clear separation of church and state is to be noted. Other points of interest will be noted shortly, but the separation of church and state in Calvin's thought is confirmed by a statement of 4:11:1 of the *Institutes*. "For as no city or town can exist without a magistracy and civil polity, so the Church of God, as I have already stated, but am now obliged to repeat, stands in need of a certain spiritual polity; which, however, is entirely distinct from the civil polity." Calvin's comments on Matthew 22:15–22 also confirm this point.

4. Calvin for the Unity of Church and State

While Calvin coordinated, limited, and in some sense, separated church and state, we are not to think of this separation in the modern, and certainly not in the secular, sense of separation of church and state. Spykman cites H. Van Til, who well summarizes Calvin's perspective:

> Calvin saw the church and the state as two interdependent entities each having received its authority from the sovereign God. In this conception the state is never secular, nor are state and church separated in the modern sense of the word. Atheistic democracy and popular sovereignty cannot claim Calvin as their father. According to Calvin, church and state must live in peace and must cooperate together in subjection to the Word of God. Each is to have its own jurisdiction. The state has authority in purely civil and temporal matters; the church in spiritual matters.[62]

It may be that for neither Christian nor secular modern man, Calvin has adequately separated church and state. His use of the soul and body analogy, a stock image of medieval scholasticism for the relation of church and state, marks the medieval character of his thought and his assumption of the medieval synthesis of society. This is visible in quotations given above from 3:19:15 and 4:11:1 of the *Institutes*. But the use of this analogy is clearest in the opening paragraph of the closing chapter of this work entitled "On Civil Government." Picking one statement among several,

---

62   Holwerda, 198f.

we may quote Calvin as saying, "But he who knows how to distinguish between the body and the soul . . . will find no difficulty
in understanding, that the spiritual kingdom of Christ and civil
government are things very different and remote from each other"
(4:20:1). This is an interesting case of Calvin taking a medieval
analogy and applying it for a very non-medieval purpose.

The other place at which Calvin assumes clearly a medieval view
of society as "Corpus Christianum" is in his insistence that it is the
business of the government of the state to enforce conformity to
the true religion (4:20:3, 9 of the *Institutes*). This is the element
of truth in Bainton's quip to the effect that if Calvin ever wrote
anything in favor of toleration, it was a typographical error![63]

Spykman's conclusion to his informative article on "Sphere
Sovereignty in Calvin and the Calvinist Tradition" well summarizes the debt modern democracy owes to Calvin:

> We find in Calvin a decisive departure from earlier
> Constantinian-medieval views of society, based
> upon the nature-grace dichotomy, and structured
> along the lines of the principle of sphere-subsidiarity
> with church and state alternatingly pressing their
> sovereign claims on other institutions in society.
>
> Calvin gave us a breakaway from the Scholastic
> principle of sphere-subsidiarity and a breakthrough
> toward the Reformed principle of sphere-sovereignty.
> All that remained was to develop a more consistent
> follow-through.[64]

B. His View of the Ideal Form of Government

When one takes up Calvin's views on the proper form of government, one must never forget that for Calvin this was a secondary, circumstantial, and speculative issue. This he makes clear in

63   *Calvin and Calvinism*, 16.
64   Holwerda, ed., *Exploring the Heritage of John Calvin*, 207–208.

4:20:7–8 of the *Institutes*. Yet in that very section of the *Institutes*, he makes clear there are principles that every form of government should ideally conform to. He says, "I readily acknowledge that no kind of government is more happy than this, where liberty is regulated with becoming moderation, and properly established on a durable basis, so also I consider those as the most happy people, who are permitted to enjoy such a condition" (4:20:8). McNeill comments on Calvin's love of liberty:

> If we test a writer's attitude to democracy by his references to "liberty, equality, and fraternity," we find Calvin highly positive on the first and last of these: . . . In his *Homilies on 1 Samuel* he . . . twice refers to liberty as "an inestimable good." The Hebrew people, prizing too lightly this priceless boon, lost it when they demanded a king. Liberty is something to be held in the highest esteem and to be strenuously maintained. On the passage, "Rejoice Zebulun in thy going out and Issachar in thy tents" (Deut. 33:18), Calvin pours contempt upon Issachar as a type of those who though strong and able, lose liberty through faintheartedness and sloth. Commenting on Deut. 24:7, he speaks of liberty as "more than the half of life." There is no doubt about Calvin's espousal of liberty.[65]

It is this love of liberty that may be discerned in 4:20:31 of the *Institutes* in Calvin's famous sentences regarding the "magistrates of the people." Surely there is the implied suggestion in these sentences that ideally such magistrates ought to exist in every civil polity. Such checks on supreme authority are necessary because of human depravity. This Calvin makes clear in 4:20:8 of the *Institutes*: "The vice or imperfection of men therefore renders it safer and more tolerable for the government to be in the hands of many, . . . and that if any one arrogate to himself more than is right, the many may act as censors and masters to restrain his ambition."

---

65   *Calvin and Calvinism*, 33.

It is something as basic as Calvin's doctrine of human depravity—of which no one's was stronger—that led him to oppose monarchy and prefer "either aristocracy, or a mixture of aristocracy and democracy." This well-known sentiment is stated also in 4:20:8 of the *Institutes*. It is not easy to overstate Calvin's hatred of monarchy, an antipathy that seems to have grown with the experiences of his later life. His commentary on Daniel from this period of his life is filled with anti-monarchical sentiment (see his comments on Dan. 3:13–15; 6:3–5–7). McNeill offers this summary of Calvin's feelings on this matter:

> Among the forms of government Calvin sometimes professes indifference on theoretical grounds, but on grounds of history and experience he exhibits a sharp dislike of kingship. His *Sermons on Job* (1554) contain lists of the offenses characteristic of the behavior of kings. The *Sermons on Deuteronomy* (155455) present sweeping denunciations of royal wickedness. In his *Lectures on Daniel* (1561) he observes the sacrilegious pride, susceptibility to flattery and other faults of King Darius, and regards these as characteristic of monarchs and accentuated in modern princes. "We today may well weep," he writes, "over the heartlessness of kings," and "over the condition of the world" in which they bear sway. "If one could uncover the hearts of kings, he would find hardly one in a hundred who does not likewise despise everything divine.[66]

We may conclude this argument for the view that modem democracy owes a debt to Calvin for its cherished possession of limited government confident that the international movement issuing from Calvin's Geneva carried in its bosom a delight in liberty and a theory of limited government that it owed to Calvin himself. Here at least the roots of modern democracy are deep in the soil of Calvinism!

---

66   *Calvin and Calvinism*, 30.

IV. CALVINISM'S ADOPTION OF THE DISTINCTIVE TENETS OF THE SOCIAL CONTRACT THEORY

In taking up this subject, it must be said at the outset that no thorough treatment of this vast subject is intended. The positions defended thus far form, however, a kind of prolegomena to this subject and demand at least a suggestive treatment.

Another problem that exacerbates the difficulty of this subject is that most scholars who write about the political views of Calvin's contemporaries and successors do not have as the basis of their studies the clearly defined view of Calvin's political perspectives this paper has defended. Their treatment of the relation of the views of Calvin to the views of his contemporaries tend, therefore, to be confused. Wherever there is not a clearly defined appreciation of Calvin's anti-revolutionary stance, such confusion will be unavoidable.

Certain general conclusions do, however, follow from the positions here maintained when they are compared with the political views of Calvin's successors. These conclusions may now be stated.

A. The Reality of Calvinism's Adoption of the Distinctive Tenets of the Social Contract Theory

It scarcely needs to be argued that if Calvin's political views are what this treatment has said they are, then later Calvinism drastically departed from Calvin's views. It is no secret that the social contract theory was adopted by Calvin's successors in all its main features. The culmination of this process of departure from Calvin's political views is certainly reached in Samuel Rutherford's *Lex Rex*, published in 1644, eighty years after Calvin's death. One may trace Rutherford's positions to much earlier writers, but his work may serve as an undeniable illustration of the process in question. John Legg has helpfully summarized the main positions defended by Rutherford. He says,

Rutherford argues that the power of government (not governing) rests in *the people, who may choose* to appoint one or more to rule over the nation. Although God ordains all rulers in his providence, and may actually, as with many Old Testament kings, declare his choice, it nevertheless lies with the people to elect or make the king. . . . On this basis Rutherford then asserts that the relation between king and people is one of covenant. . . . According to the law of nature, the people cannot give away their rights absolutely and unconditionally. The safety of the people is the supreme rule and this is why they appoint a king. . . . Again the practical implication is clear. What the people give, the people can take away.

Legg then quotes Rutherford himself:

Page 132 states the argument in a different and very vivid manner: "If I give my sword to my fellow to defend me from the murderer, if he shall fall to and murder me with my own sword, I may (if I have the strength) take my sword from him." If the ruler breaks the covenant, he forfeits his rights and may be deposed. Although this would usually be the task of inferior rulers, Rutherford does not limit it to them.

Legg then summarizes Rutherford's political views in a short paragraph:

Putting the three principles together, we arrive at the conclusion that since rulers are God's ministers appointed through men, they must rule according to God's will for the benefit of the people. When they fail to do so they may and must be resisted by disobedience, protest, flight, and, in the end, force. If the rulers persist in such failure, so that their whole rule becomes a tyranny, they may be deposed, either by inferior rulers or by the people, if they have the necessary strength.[67]

Such teaching is a whole world away from Calvin's political commitments. It is true, of course, that Calvin appears to have exercised a moderating influence on the Calvinistic revolutionary tradition. This is evident even in Rutherford in at least two ways. There is, first, a general reticence to resort to revolution except as a last resort in extreme situations. There is, second, a general insistence that revolution be led by inferior magistrates. This second moderating influence is more evident in earlier writers.[68] In Rutherford, this insistence has been reduced to a mere preference.

Though the fact of divergence from Calvin by the Calvinistic tradition is clear, it would be very difficult to trace the exact steps in the process that led to this total reversal by the Calvinistic tradition on the subject of the social contract and revolution. Skinner attempts this task in his *Calvinism and the Theory of Revolution*. This work is marred by a failure to clearly appreciate the depth and consistency of Calvin's anti-revolutionary principles.[69] Nonetheless, he may be correct in tracing the beginnings of this development to Beza's sympathy for popular sovereignty, though he points out that Beza rejected any revolution not led by the inferior magistrates.[70] As was noted already, Kingdon believes there is evidence that Beza was far more sympathetic to the conspiracy of Amboise.[71] Gosselin believes that he discerns vacillation in Beza's political views with Calvin exercising a moderating influence upon him.[72] It seems safe to conclude that Beza occupies a conservative and mediating position with reference to the later radical development of the Calvinistic political theory. He toyed

---

67   Legg, 12, 13, 16.
68   Skinner, 331.
69   Skinner, 192, 214, 220.
70   Skinner, 306f.
71   Kingdon, "The Political Resistance of the Calvinists," 224.
72   E. A. Gosselin, "David in Tempore Belli: Beza's David in the Service of the Huguenots," *Sixteenth Century Journal* (1976), 7:36–50.

with popular sovereignty, rejected popular revolution demanding that it be led by inferior magistrates, removed Calvin's doubts as to the existence of "magistrates of the people" in France, and allowed magistrates far more inferior than Calvin would have been happy with to lead armed resistance.

Robert D. Linder has studied Pierre Viret's political thought in his *Pierre Viret and the Sixteenth Century French Protestant Revolutionary Tradition*.[73] He has failed to prove to this writer and to many other of his reviewers that Viret's views differed substantively from Calvin. It does seem to be safe to conclude, however, that Viret was far more vociferous in his attacks on tyranny and far more liberal in the general emphasis of his political teaching. He may in this way have contributed to the Calvinistic revolutionary tradition.

We may discern in Beza and Viret the first indications of drift from Calvin's position. This drift becomes a turbulent current in the writings of Hotman, Ponet, Mornay, and especially the writings from across the English Channel of Goodman, Knox, and Buchanan. As was noted, the conflict between Calvin and Knox on this issue was visible already in the lifetime of Calvin.[74]

B. *The Sources of Calvinism's Adoption of the Distinctive Tenets of the Social Contract Theory*

The question naturally arises, If Calvin himself is not the source of Calvinistic revolutionary tradition, where did it come from? We have already noted the long tradition of political views substantially the same as those of the later social contract theory and its legitimation of revolution.[75] Skinner notes that such theories appealed to some Lutheran writers and are adopted in the Magdeburg Confession.[76] Bucer, of wide influence in Reformed Protestant

---

73   R. D. Linder, "Pierre Viret and the Sixteenth-Century French Protestant Revolutionary Tradition," *The Journal of Modern History* (1966), 38:125–137.
74   Calvin, 7:47.
75   *Calvin and Calvinism*, 51; see also Mueller, 153; Skinner, 321f.; Waskey, 224.
76   Skinner, 200, 209.

circles, was influenced by such thinking.[77] Though our study shows that Calvin resisted any revolutionary tendencies in Bucer, it may well be that others developed tendencies of a revolutionary nature.

Given his confusion concerning the thought of Calvin himself, one is somewhat surprised that Skinner, in tracing the revolutionary tendencies of Calvinism to non-Calvinistic and even non-Christian sources, states the conclusion that the evidence presented in this treatment surely warrants.

> The Jesuit Mariana may thus be said to link hands with the Protestant Buchanan in stating a theory of popular sovereignty which, while scholastic in its origins and Calvinist in its later development, was in essence independent of either religious creed, and was thus available to be used by all parties in the coming constitutional struggles of the seventeenth century.[78]

Skinner goes on to call the theory he is discussing "purely secular" and "wholly populist." Believing that Calvin accurately represented the biblical attitude toward social contract theory, we are ready to agree with Skinner's words, though in a sense he did not intend.

C. The Rationale of Calvinism's Adoption of the Distinctive Tenets of the Social Contract Theory

In speaking of the reality and the sources of Calvinistic adoption of the social contract theory, we have not yet explained why Calvinism so readily accepted a theory so contrary to Calvin and the biblical view he stood for. One reason is not difficult to find. The evidence for Calvin's hostility to any form of human absolutism has already been surveyed. There was, then, a certain affinity with a theory that also opposed the rising absolutism of the European monarchies. A second reason is also not difficult to

---

77   Skinner, 205. *Calvin and Calvinism*, 50–55.
78   Skinner, 347.

locate. Calvinism as a minority faith without the protection of the constituted government was subject to constant persecution. This clearly tended to make a theory that justified revolutionary activity acceptable to many individuals in the Calvinistic movement.

These factors led to an historic alliance between Calvinism and Renaissance humanism. Hans Baron has accurately portrayed this alliance:

> For Protestantism, this question was a vital problem. All the great monarchs, who were the overlords of Spain and Italy, of France and Germany, of Scotland and of the Netherlands, and to a certain extent even the English kings, became close allies of reinvigorated Catholicism. Complete victory of the absolute monarchy would have meant the extinction of the Reformation everywhere. The starting points for the new religion, on the other hand, were individual local circles—estates, cities, provinces, (like the Netherlands), or papers of the civic element and the nobility. A natural alliance was to link the Reformation with the opponents of centralizing absolutism. The political struggles of the cities and estates for the defence of their liberty gained a new background, a higher motive, in the defence of religion. . . . What we know as the political doctrine of Calvin and so many of his followers had been the product of an historic cooperation of Protestant religion and the civic world of the city-state. The new outlook of politics in a religious guise had been older than Calvin. It had originated at the very moment when the civic element of the Renaissance period and the new religion had joined forces for the first time.[79]

Though Baron is wrong in identifying Calvin's political views with those of his followers and of Bucer, his grasp of the alliance

---

79 *Calvin and Calvinism,* 52, 54.

between two distinct worldviews that took place in the crucible of the embattled independent cities of Europe's sixteenth century is very instructive.

V. CONCLUSIONS

A. *The Causes of the Calvin Political Debate*

We conclude, as we began this chapter, by asserting that the causes of the Calvin political debate are not to be traced to equivocation in the teaching of Calvin himself. We have shown that there is a remarkable consistency in Calvin's political views throughout all his writings and his life. The debate stems, rather, from two failures on the part of Calvin scholars. There has been the failure to adequately distinguish between Calvin and later Calvinism as to their complete diversity on the subject of the social contract theory and revolution. While Calvin's anti-totalitarian views were maintained with growing vigor, his rejection of revolution was forgotten. There has also been the failure on the part of modern scholars to adequately appreciate that two distinct movements are allied in modern democracy: the Calvinistic teaching of limited government and the humanistic teaching of the social contract theory. When revolutionary theory and limited government are made the twin pillars of modern democracy, as Hudson does,[80] it is impossible to give a simple answer to the question, Was Calvin the founder of modern democracy? For, while Calvin was, arguably, the one who gave Western civilization the gift of limited government, he opposed with his whole might the revolutionary tendencies of the social contract theory.

We can now discern why Calvin has seemed to equivocate on political matters in the view of modern scholars. They themselves have been guilty of the equivocation of reading later Calvinism back into Calvin and of the equivocation of not distinguishing the two diverse allies responsible for giving us the system of modern democracy.

---

80   *Calvin and Calvinism,* 18.

B. The Lessons of Calvin for Twentieth-century Christian Political Activism

The thought of Calvin confronts us with several important lessons that must be underscored briefly.

Political righteousness is not the condition of legitimacy for any political entity. Civil authority is to retain our subjection, though not our obedience, whether it is in our estimation measuring up to our standards of political righteousness.

Christianity, then, never permits terrorism or revolution in the proper sense of those terms. Political force and resistance to tyranny may only be used by civil authorities charged to protect our freedoms as a people. Theologies of Liberation that do not recognize the peculiar providential legitimation of any existing government would meet Calvin's unalloyed rejection.

Political righteousness remains, notwithstanding what has just been said, the unavoidable concern of a Calvinistic Christian. The sovereign God's claims through His Word on human society are totalitarian.

Our study reminds us that we may not equate the American system of government with ideal, biblical governmental forms. This is not to gainsay the undoubted influence of Calvinism on our governmental form. It is only to remember that it was not the only influence.

C. The Rejection of the Doctrine of Just Revolution by the Central Figure of the Reformed Tradition

It needs no proving that Calvin is the central figure of the Reformed tradition. Further, it requires no demonstration that he believed that all kings and civil magistrates are subject to God and His Word as the norm for their official duties. Calvin, it has been shown, even thought it the magistrate's responsibility to support the true religion. Never did he, however, infer from this the doctrine of just revolution. Always he rejected any and all theories of just revolution.

The position that thinks of the doctrine of just revolution as "Reformed" must ignore Calvin to do so. The logic that deduces just revolution from the sovereignty of God's Word must find Calvin illogical. The exegesis that promotes just revolution must reject Calvin's exegesis as pervasively unacceptable.

Part 2

BIBLICAL CRITIQUE

Chapter 3

From Theocracy to Autocracy: The Relation of the People of God to Civil Authority in the Transitional Period Surrounding the Exile

The purpose of this chapter is to elucidate the changing relations of the people of God to civil authority in that critical and transitional period of the Old Testament marked by the Babylonian exile. The meaningful accomplishment of this task requires an examination of more than merely the relations of the people of God to the Gentile kings placed over them, though this is central. This period must be contrasted with and placed in the context of the theocratic kingdom that both precedes and succeeds it and which it interrupts. A functional understanding of the theocracy and its relationship to the Gentile kingdoms is, thus, imperative. This chapter, therefore, proposes to examine, first, the disruption of the theocratic kingdom and then the authority of the Gentile kingdoms.

This chapter functions in the thesis as an introduction to the New Testament teaching as to the duty of subordination to and the prohibition of rebellion against civil authority. It does so, by examining the transition to the historical political situation in which the church must function, by explaining the duties required of the people of God in that situation, and thus by providing the redemptive-historical backdrop for the New Testament teaching regarding civil authority.

I. THE DISRUPTION OF THE THEOCRATIC KINGDOM

A. The Nature of the Theocracy

Any treatment of the disruption of the theocratic kingdom confronts, first of all, the task of defining the term, *theocracy*. Though this term is a venerable part of theological vocabulary, exactly defining it is difficult. Not that its meaning etymologically or superficially is in doubt. Etymologically, it is "God-rule." Webster, recognizing its native, civil context, properly defines it as "the rule of a state by God or a god."[1]

When one attempts a theological or biblical definition, however, problems arise. *Theocracy* is not a biblical word. Josephus seems to have coined it.[2] Worse yet, *theocracy* is a loaded word with a long history in theological controversy. The purpose of this treatment (thankfully) does not demand anything like an exhaustive study of the term. Nonetheless some clarity must be introduced into the way it will be used in this paper.

Webster's definition, while accurate, lacks clarity. The Bible's most basic teaching regarding civil government is that it owes its origin to God and is accountable to him (Ps 82:1f.; Rom 13:1f.; 1 Pet 2:13f.). Thus, Webster's definition might permit us to regard every state as a theocracy. Yet, if anything is clear, it is that something more distinctive, more unique, is meant by the term. This brings us to the first and controlling aspect of the definition of *theocracy*.

1. *Yahveh is in a unique sense king of Israel.* There ought to be

---

1   *Webster's New World Dictionary* (World, 1966), s.v. "theocracy."
2   G. F. Oehler, *Theology of the Old Testament*, trans by G. E. Day (Minneapolis, Klock & Klock, 1987), 199. See also W. M. McPheeters, *International Standard Bible Encyclopedia*, ed. J. Orr, V (Wilmington, AP&A, n.d), 2965.

nothing startling in God's claim to be king. As Creator, He is sovereign of all (Ps 74; 93:2; 103:19f). It is not, however, merely this dominion that God claims when He proclaims himself king of Israel, and thus, it is not merely this general dominion the term *theocracy* designates. For God's kingship in Israel is specifically the proper starting point of both Josephus' use of the word and its precise, theological use.[3] Oehler's words need some qualification, but as a starting point for the definition of *theocracy*, they are accurate: "The Old Testament idea of the divine kingship expresses, not God's general relation of power toward the world (as being its creator and supporter), but the special relation of His government toward His elect people."[4] This meaning of God's kingship pervades the Old Testament and is a prominent characterization of His peculiar relation to Israel (Ps 44:1–8, esp. v. 4; Ps 68, esp. v. 24; Isa 41:21). Perhaps this becomes most pointed when Yahveh is viewed as the commander of Israel's army (Exod 12:41; 17:8–16; Num 10:35; 21:14; 23:21).

Yahveh's assumption of kingship over Israel is related to the exodus period in Israel's history, and most specifically to the covenant-making at Sinai. Deuteronomy 33:1–5 is the *locus classicus* here. It identifies the commencement of Yahveh's kingship with the Sinai covenant-making. Note in particular the reference to the covenant meal with Israel's leaders in verse 5. This is a reference to events recorded in Exodus 24:1–12. Isaiah in his discussion of the new exodus refers frequently to the original exodus as the period of Israel's (national) creation. Isaiah 43:15 thus identifies Yahveh's kingship with this period: "I am Yahveh, your Holy One, the Creator of Israel, your King." In a similar manner, Yahveh's kingship over Israel is closely related to His being Israel's redeemer, a designation that clearly recalls the exodus period. Such references give a broader and more dynamic view of Yahveh's kingship over Israel and its origin but one that nonetheless corroborates the idea that Yahveh's kingship over Israel and the Sinai covenant are

3   McPheeters, 2965.
4   Oehler, *Theology of the Old Testament*, 199.

inextricably related (Ps 10:16). Oehler comments, "The Patriarchs called Him Lord and Shepherd, and it is not until He has formed for Himself a people by bringing Israel up out of Egypt that He is called, Exod. 5:18, 'He who is King forever and ever.'"[5] This makes sense. It is only a nation over which one may be king (not the head of a family or clan.)[6]

The natural conclusion one may draw from all this is that God would occupy the place human kings occupied in other nations. One might think such a conclusion simplistic. He might also wonder how this exactly relates to the Davidic kingship later instituted and previously prophesied. Nonetheless, this is precisely the conclusion the pervasive teaching of the Old Testament demands we draw. Yahveh occupied just the place human kings did in other commonwealths (Judg 8:23; 1 Sam 8, 12:12; 2 Chr 13:8). This is also implied by the defect, humanly speaking, of the Mosaic civil order in that no definite office of executive power is appointed at the exodus period. Oehler comments, "The Mosaic Theocracy presents the peculiar phenomenon of being originally unprovided with a definite office for executing the power of the state."[7] We may conclude with the words of McPheeters:

> If the foregoing be a correct account of the idea expressed by the word "theocracy" and particularly if the foregoing be a correct account of the O. T. representation of God's relation to, and rule in and over Israel, it follows as a matter of course that the realization of such an idea was only possible within the sphere of what is known as special revelation. Indeed, special revelation of the Divine will, through Divinely chosen organs, to Divinely appointed

---

5 Oehler, 199.

6 One cannot forebear mentioning the correlation of all this with the idea that the old covenant is patterned on the ancient, suzerainty treaties of the kings of the Near East popularized by Meredith Kline. Note his *Treaty of the Great King* (Grand Rapids, Eerdmans, 1963).

7 Oehler, 199.

executive agents, is, itself, the very essence of the idea of theocracy.[8]

2. *The direct promulgation by special revelation of a specific and detailed civil order is characteristic of the theocratic order.*

As a matter of fact, it is precisely this divinely revealed civil order that is often in mind when the term *theocracy* is used. It is both interesting and appropriate in light of what has just been said about the formal assumption of kingship over Israel by Yahveh at Sinai that the giving of this civil law-order occupies a prominent place in the Sinaitic covenant. This becomes clear in all sorts of ways. Deuteronomy 33:1–5 specifically mentions as part and parcel of Yahveh's kingship "the law that Moses gave us, the possession of the assembly of Jacob." The contextual reference makes it impossible in the light of that historical record to exclude a reference here to the "Book of the Covenant," the epitome of the civil law-order of Israel. Also interesting is the reference to the law as the possession of "the assembly of Jacob," a reference to Israel as a formal, civil (as well as religious) entity.

All this already implies the prominence of this civil law-order in the exodus account. Immediately after the speaking of the Ten words by God Himself, Exodus 20, but before the ratification of the covenant by blood and the covenant meal in chapter 24 (Heb. 9:18f.), there intervenes the promulgation of the divine civil law-order of the theocratic kingdom in chapters 21–23. These chapters epitomize this order. Note Hebrews 9:19: "When Moses had proclaimed *every commandment of the law* to all the people, he took the blood." This is not to say that this civil law-order is not later expanded. It is to say that Exodus 21–23 is the epitome of this order. The civil character of the laws of 21:1–23:13 is evident from even a cursory reading.

This brief exposition of the prominence of a divinely revealed civil or national order in the theocracy may be concluded by a reference to Deuteronomy 4:5–8:

8 McPheeters, 2965.

> See, I have taught you statutes and judgments just as
> the LORD my God commanded me, that you should
> do thus in the land where you are entering to possess
> it. So keep and do them, for that is your wisdom and
> your understanding in the sight of the peoples who
> will hear all these statutes and say, "Surely this great
> nation is a wise and understanding people." For what
> great nation is there that has a god so near to it as
> is the LORD our God whenever we call on Him?
> Or what great nation is there that has statutes and
> judgments as righteous as this whole law which I am
> setting before you today.

It is preeminently the civil order that is in view. This is clear, first of all, from the fact that it is Israel as a nation—a civil order—contrasted with other nations that is in view. Further, the terms *statutes* and *judgments* are contrasted in Deuteronomy with the covenant itself and clearly refer to the detailed civil order to be followed in the land (Deut 4:12–14; 5:1–3 with 5:30–6:3). This civil order was one of the glories of theocratic Israel. Note Isaiah 33:22: "For the LORD is our judge, the LORD is our lawgiver, the LORD is our king: He will save us."

3. *A third characteristic of the theocracy, one which is often at the heart of its theological usage, is what may be called the union of church and state in the theocratic kingdom.* Oehler remarks, "Church and state, if we may speak thus, are here joined in immediate union."[9] Fairbairn marks this idea out as the key idea of the theocracy:

> First, then, in respect to the true idea of the
> theocracy—wherein stood its distinctive nature?
> It stood in the formal exhibition of God as King
> or Supreme Head of the commonwealth, so that
> all authority and law emanated from Him; *and, by
> necessary consequence, there were not two societies in
> the ordinary sense, civil and religious, but a fusion of*

---

9   Oehler, *Theology of the Old Testament*, 199.

> *the two into one body, or, as we might express it from*
> *a modern point of view, a merging together of Church*
> *and State.* . . . And this is simply the idea embodied
> in the Jewish theocracy; it is the fact of Yahveh
> condescending to occupy, in Israel, such a centre of
> power and authority. He proclaimed Himself "King
> in Jeshurun." Israel became the commonwealth with
> which He more peculiarly associated His presence
> and His glory. Not only the seat of His worship, but
> His throne also, was in Zion—both His sanctuary
> and His dominion.[10]

Many aspects of the civil law of Israel corroborate this observation. There were civil penalties for religious defection to idolatry and the frequent involvement of the priests and Levites in civil matters (Num 5:15f., 35, Deut 19, 21:5). Deuteronomy 23:1–8 contains ceremonial and national restrictions with strong religious overtones upon entrance into the assembly of Israel. Girdlestone comments, "The being 'cut off from the congregation of Israel,' and the being forbidden to enter it (Num. 19:20, Deut. 23:1), seem to have implied severance from the privileges, religious and social, which the nation as such enjoyed."[11]

What most insistently demands the observation under discussion is, however, the fact that the seat, center, and focus of both civil power and religious worship in Israel was identical. The ark of the covenant in the holy of holies first in the tabernacle and later in the temple was the throne of Jehovah (1 Sam 4:4; 2 Sam 6:2; 2 Kgs 19:15; 1 Chr 13:6; Ps 80:1, 99:1; Isa 37:16). This is not surprising. It was in the tabernacle and later in the temple that Yahveh dwelt with His people, Israel. If Yahveh was the king of Israel, it follows that these places must have been His throne. This temple-throne equation meets us everywhere in the Scriptures

---

10   Patrick Fairbairn, *The Typology of Scripture* (Evangelical Press, 1975), 2:418–419, emphasis his.
11   R. B. Girdlestone, *Synonyms of the Old Testament* (Grand Rapids: Eerdmans, 1986).

(Num 10:35–36; Ps 11:3; Isa 6:1f; Ezek 43:7; Jer 3:16, 17[12]). Even the identity of Israel as at one and the same time a "kingdom of priests," (Exod 19:6), points to the identity of the civil and ecclesiastical establishments since it attributes both royal and priestly status to the "holy nation."[13]

One may point, finally, to how Jerusalem under the Davidic covenant becomes the center of temple worship and, thus, the geographical locale of the throne of God. The future location of the temple is chosen by Yahveh Himself (2 Sam 24:15–25; 1 Chr 21:18–22:5). At the same time, Jerusalem becomes the seat of the line of Davidic kings with whom the theocratic kingdom is identified (2 Sam 5:7; 6:12; 1 Kgs 2:10; 8:1; 9:24). Thus, the civil and ecclesiastical are again connected.

Before taking up this fourth aspect of the theocracy, a note of qualification is in order. For notwithstanding all that has been said of the union of church and state, an element of separation remains. It is the strict separation of the royal and priestly offices. The king and the priest were never to be the same in the theocratic kingdom (1 Sam 13:8–14). This points to the ultimate inadequacy of these institutions to fulfill the theocratic ideal. It leaves the uniting point of the theocratic kingdom even in its fullest Old Testament development in the person of Yahveh. The prophets indicated all such inadequacy and imperfection will be removed in the eschaton. Of the one who perfectly united the divine and Davidic kingships, it is written, "Behold, a man whose name is Branch, . . . for He will build the temple of the LORD. Yes, it is He who will build the temple of the LORD, and He who will bear the honor and sit and rule on His throne. Thus, He will be a priest on His throne,

---

12   Keith Crim, gen. ed., *The Interpreter's Dictionary of the Bible* (Nashville: Abingdon, 1982), s.v. "theocracy."

13   Brown, Driver, Briggs, *Hebrew and English Lexicon of the Old Testament*, attributes the meaning "priest-king" to Basileion here. The LXX translates *Basileion hierateuma*, royal priesthood, and this rendering is adopted in the NT (1 Pet 2:9). Other references to this phrase in the NT further substantiate this translation (Rev 1:6; 5:10).

and the counsel of peace will be between the two offices" (Zech 6:12–13; see also Ps 110).

4. *The fourth and concluding perspective in our definition of* theocracy *is the Davidic fulfillment and mediation of the theocratic kingdom.*

The difficulty that confronts us at the outset is the reconciliation of a human king in Israel with the theocratic ideal. The evidence presented earlier for Yahveh's being in a realistic sense the king of Israel might seem to preclude the rise of a human dynasty. This problem becomes acute in 1 Samuel 8, 10, and 12. The request for a king is regarded by both Samuel and Yahveh as a rejection of Yahveh's rule.

Nonetheless it would be wrong to find in such passages the absolute prohibition of all human monarchy. The Mosaic law in Deuteronomy 17:14–20 clearly and without condemnation contemplates this occurrence. Two remarks alleviate the seeming difficulty raised by such passages: (1) The condemnation of the request for a king in 1 Samuel 8:6, 19 rests not on the fact of the request itself. Such a request is already contemplated in Deuteronomy 17:14. It is rather the spirit with which the request is made which is the objectionable thing.[14] (2) Deuteronomy 17:15 requires that Yahveh choose the human king of Israel. The spirit in which the king was requested in 1 Samuel 8 militated against the sovereign prerogative of Yahveh in this matter. This fact also explains Gideon's rejection of kingship when it was offered him (Judg 8:23). Yahveh had not chosen him for this! The Hebrew verb *bachar* used in Deuteronomy 17:15 plays a highly significant role in the development of human kingship in Israel. Samuel's use of *bachar* in reference to Saul is ambivalent. Twice, with a condemnatory emphasis, he states that Saul is the king *Israel* chose (1 Sam 8:18; 12:13)! Once he proclaims Saul the king whom Yahveh had chosen (1 Kgs 10:24). It is not wrong to see in this ambivalence

---

14 C. F. Keil, *Biblical Commentary on the Books of Samuel*, trans. by J. Martin (Grand Rapids: Eerdmans, 1975), 82–84. See also Matthew Poole, *A Commentary on the Holy Bible* (Edinburgh: Banner of Truth, 1974), 1:531.

the idea that Yahveh's choice of Saul was ultimately intended as a judgment on Israel for the spirit in which they sought a king from Samuel, the spirit of rebellion and distrust (Hos 8:4; 9:9; 13:10).

In contrast, the use of *bachar* with reference to Yahveh's choice of David is frequent and unqualified (1 Kgs 8:16; 11:34; 1 Chr 28:4–6; Ps 78:67f.; 1 Sam 16:8f.; 2 Chr 6:6; Ps 89:19f). This establishes that no ultimate conflict existed between a human king and the theocratic ideal. The evidence for the Davidic mediation of the theocratic kingdom, now to be examined, further corroborates this assertion.

a. The Direct Statements of the Davidic Mediation of the Theocratic Kingdom

The Chronicler has for one of his motifs the idea that Yahveh's kingship is now exercised through the Davidic dynasty. First Chronicles 17:14 lays the foundation for the development of this theme in its record of the Davidic covenant itself. Through Nathan, Yahveh says of David's son, "But I will settle him in My house and My kingdom forever and his throne shall be established forever." First Chronicles 28:5 records David's proclamation of the Solomonic succession: "He [Yahveh] has chosen my son Solomon to sit on the throne of the kingdom of the LORD over Israel." First Chronicles 29:23 records the second inauguration of Solomon as king. "Then Solomon sat on the throne of the LORD as king." Second Chronicles 13:8 records Abijah's speech to Jehoram and all Israel. While Abijah's historical account may be slanted, the theology of verse 8 is unimpeachable: "So now you intend to resist the kingdom of the LORD through [in the hands of] the sons of David."

b. The Symbolic Identification of the Divine Throne with the Davidic Throne

The ark of the covenant, as already remarked, was the throne of Yahveh. It is of intense interest, then, when both 2 Samuel 6 and 1 Chronicles 15 and 16 record the bringing of the ark of God to

Jerusalem immediately prior to the divine establishment of the Davidic dynasty. Second Samuel 6:2 emphasizes the royal significance of the ark: "the ark of God which is called by the Name, the very Name of the LORD of hosts who is enthroned above the cherubim." Given the specific provisions of the Davidic covenant, the clear, though figurative, meaning of this event is the identification of the divine throne with the Davidic throne. There is the symbolic identification of the divine throne with the Davidic throne, in 2 Samuel 6, just as there is the covenantal identification in 2 Samuel 7. O. Palmer Robertson remarks, "David brought the ark of God to Jerusalem (2 Samuel 6). In so doing he publicly displayed his desire to see his own rule in Israel related immediately to the throne of God. In this manner, the concept of the Theocracy found its fullest expression."[15]

c. The Organic Relation of the Sinaitic Covenant and the Davidic Covenant

The very context of the Davidic covenant contains indication of this organic relation. Second Samuel 7:1 states of David that "the LORD had given him rest on every side from all his enemies." It ought to need no proof that the whole point of the Sinaitic covenant was to give Israel rest (cf. the use of *nuach*, the verb in 2 Sam 7:1, in both Exod 20:8–11 and Deut 5:14 as well as in Deut 12:10 because of its parallels with 2 Sam 7:1f). The message of this notation in 2 Samuel 7:1 is that in David and the Davidic covenant, the Sinaitic covenant finds both its continuation and culmination.[16]

The Davidic covenant is tied to the Sinaitic covenant not only in terms of its blessings but also in terms of its laws. Clearly, as chief executive officer of the state, the king would be responsible for the implementation of the theocratic civil law. Deuteronomy

---

15 O. Palmer Robertson, *The Christ of the Covenants* (Grand Rapids, Baker Book House, 1980), 230. See also Oehler, *Theology of the Old Testament*, 199.

16 Robertson, *The Christ of the Covenants*, 231.

17:14–20 specifically mentions in verses 18–20 the requirement that the king write and study and observe the law. The civil law of Israel would undoubtedly be included in such a manuscript, and it is at least possible that the "Book of the Covenant" Exodus 21–23, is specifically in view.[17] This responsibility to keep the law of Moses is spelled out in two crucial passages regarding Solomon in 1 Kings: first in David's dying charge to Solomon (21:4) and then in Yahveh's second appearance to Solomon after the dedication of the temple (9:1–9). (See also the example of Josiah in 2 Kgs 22:1–23:30 and 2 Chr 34 and 35.)

Such data requires the rejection of all divorcing of the Davidic covenant and Mosaic covenant, whether exegetically or theologically motivated.[18] Their organic relation must be maintained!

d. The Specific Provisions of the Davidic Covenant

The high point of the evidence for the Davidic mediation of the theocratic kingdom is found in the provisions of the Davidic covenant itself:

- David's Son/God's Son

Perhaps the clearest indication of the unification of the divine and Davidic thrones is Yahveh's adoption of David's son and heir (2 Sam 7:14; 1 Chr 17:14; Ps 89:26–29; 2:2–7). Davidic royalty becomes divine royalty. Oehler remarks,

> The theocratic king is the son of God, the firstborn among the kings of the earth. . . . By sonship is expressed chiefly the relation of love and faithfulness in which God stands to the ruler of His people. The significance of sonship must not be limited to this; but the term further implies that the king is in this capacity begotten of God, . . . that his dignity is of

---

17   P. C. Craigie, *The Book of Deuteronomy* (Grand Rapids: Eerdmans, 1976), 256.

18   Robertson, *The Christ of the Covenants*, 243–249.

Divine origin, his sovereignty a reflection of the Divine glory.[19]

The fulfillment of all this in the One who is both "David's son and David's Lord" is too clear to miss.[20]

- God's House/David's House

Robertson's comments on the interrelationships here must be quoted at length:

> One of the most striking aspects structurally of II Samuel 7 is the inversion of phrases as a mode of emphasis. This particular manner of expression brings into closest relationship the concept of "dynasty" and "dwelling-place."
>
> First, God responds with emphasis to David's proposal: "Shall you . . . build a house . . . for me?" (v. 5). Shall you, a mortal man, determine the permanent dwelling-place for the Almighty? Then God inverts the pattern of thought: "Yahveh makes known to you that he, the Lord himself, will make for you a house" (v. 11). . . . Obviously the house which the Lord shall build for David is not a royal palace, since David already lived in a "house of cedar" (v. 2). David understands God's reference to the "house" to be to his posterity: "You have spoken concerning your servant's house for a great while to come" (v. 19).
>
> David shall not build God's "house," but God shall build David's "house." The inversion of phrases interchanges "dwelling-place" with "dynasty." In both cases, perpetuity is the point of emphasis. David wishes to establish for God a permanent dwelling-place in Israel. God declares that he shall establish the perpetual dynasty of David.

---

19   Robertson, 243–249.
20   Robertson, 233f.

In his gracious words to David, God indicates that
these two "permanencies" shall be linked together. He
shall establish David's dynasty, and David's dynasty
shall establish his permanent dwelling-place. But the
order of grace must be maintained. First, the Lord
sovereignly establishes David's dynasty; then the
dynasty of David shall establish the Lord's dwelling-
place (v. 13).

The net effect of this close interchange on the basis
of the "house" figure is to bind David's rule to God's
rule, and vice versa. God shall maintain his permanent
dwelling-place as king in Israel through the kingship
of the Davidic line.[21]

This connection between God's house and David's house leads
to the two most pivotal promises of the Davidic covenant. According to Robertson, they are as follows: "One promise concerns the
line of David, and one promise concerns the locality of Jerusalem,
. . . David's line and Jerusalem's throne."[22]

All of this reconfirms the mediatorial capacity of the Davidic
kings in the theocratic kingdom of Yahveh. David's royal house
will build God's royal house. God's throne and David's throne are
geographically identified in Jerusalem.

In concluding both this treatment of the Davidic mediation
of the theocratic kingdom and the large subject of the identity of
the theocracy, one must note how by God's sovereign choice, the
theocratic kingdom has been united to the line of David and the
city of Jerusalem (Ps 78:67–72). The theocracy has been concentrated into God's choice of David and Zion. It is for their sakes
that Judah is spared time and again (1 Kgs 11:11–13, 32, 34, 36;

---

21 Robertson, 232–233. It is striking also that his interrelationship
between God's house and David's house is foreshadowed in Deut
12:11 and 17:15, which speak respectively of "place" (for worship) and
the "king" "which the LORD your God shall choose."

22 Robertson, 236.

14:21; 15:4; 2 Kgs 8:19; 19:34; 20:6).[23] It is in David and Zion that God's unique kingship over Israel is exercised, that God's specially revealed civil order is maintained, and that the union of the civil and ecclesiastical (the royal and the priestly) institutions are epitomized.

B. The Destruction of the Theocracy

The data so far presented permits the following definition of the theocracy: the theocracy is the nation of Israel as constituted by the institutions and blessings of the Sinaitic and Davidic covenants made with them by Yahveh, their king. The destruction of the theocracy implies, therefore, nothing less than the destruction of the nation of Israel. It implies the reversal of the Sinaitic covenant and the Davidic covenant, the removal of the peculiar institutions and blessings granted to Israel under these covenants. The land, the laws, the temple, the Davidic dynasty, Zion—all go in the destruction of the theocracy.

Such terminology as "the reversal of the Davidic and Sinaitic covenants" ought to remind us that the destruction of the theocracy is neither absolute nor unqualified nor permanent. How could it be? The covenants are the historical administration of the purpose of Him who has said, "My purpose will be established, and I will accomplish all My good pleasure" (Isa 46:10). If the old covenant is broken, a new and better covenant will be made (Jer. 31:31–34). If the Davidic crown is now profaned, David will yet reign in Jerusalem (Ps 89:39; Ezek 34:24.) With these qualifications, however, one may yet speak of the reversal of the theocratic blessings. The land, the great blessing secured by the old covenant, vomits out Israel and Judah! The Davidic line of kings, after reigning four hundred years in Jerusalem, the throne-city of God, forfeits its sovereignty. The reversal of the Sinaitic and the Davidic covenants must now be briefly surveyed.

---

23 Robertson, 236–240.

1.THE REVERSAL OF THE SINAITIC COVENANT

a. The Covenant Broken

Deuteronomy forecasts the eventual breaking of the covenant by Israel. Deuteronomy 29:25 records the answer to the question, "Why has the LORD done thus to this land?" (v. 24) It is "because they forsook the covenant." Therefore "the LORD uprooted them from their land" (v. 28). Deuteronomy 31:14–22 contains Yahveh's prophecy that Israel "will forsake Me and break My covenant," "spurn Me and break My covenant," and they will be "consumed" (vv. 16, 17, 20).

The accuracy of this forecast is vindicated by Jeremiah who uses the imagery of divorce (3:1–8; 31:31, 32) and rejected silver (6:27–30) to teach the formal renunciation of Judah in the exile (Ezek 16:59; 20:37).

The national and civil character of the sin that violated the covenant—as well as its religious and idolatrous character—is made ringingly clear. Jeremiah condemns the people (9:1–6), but more often, the civil rulers, "the shepherds" (Jer. 10:21; 12:10; 23:1f.; 25:34). One could add here the civil transgressions of the kings, but this will be considered later.

b. The Curse Fulfilled

The breaking of the covenant is attended by the coming of curse-signs in Deuteronomy. Foremost of these curses is the exile. Israel will perish from the land and be left few in number among the nations (Deut 4:26–27; 8:19–20; 11:17; 28:21, 36, 48, 62; 29:28; 30:18). Second Chronicles and Jeremiah record the numerous exiles and catastrophes of Judah culminating in the assassination of even Gedaliah and the flight to Egypt of the remnant that had gathered under him. Such records are the account of the overflowing fulfillment of the covenant curse.

Specific details of God's curse are given in Deuteronomy, and these find their mate in Jeremiah's prophecy. God will withhold the rain that waters Canaan (cf. Deut. 11:17; 28:23f. with Jer 14:1, 22; 3:3.) Siege conditions will lead to grotesque cannibalism (cf. Deut 28:52–57, 63, 64, with Jer 4:8; 5:8, 19–22). In general, lives filled with terror will be the portion of Israel (Deut 28:25, 37, 66f.; 32:25). "Terror on every side" is the refrain of Jeremiah's prophecies (6:25; 20:3, 4, 10; 46:5; 49:29; Lam 2:22).

2. THE REVERSAL OF THE DAVIDIC COVENANT

The pivotal promises or blessings conferred on the nation by the Davidic covenant were the Davidic dynasty, the Solomonic temple, and the unification of David's throne with God's throne in the locality of Jerusalem. Though perhaps no covenant contains such strong notes of certainty, stability, security, and what one may even call unconditionality, the Davidic covenant itself contains the intimation that all would not be continuous and undeviating progress and blessing (2 Sam 7:14; Ps 89:30–37).

The literature of the Old Testament lays the responsibility for the demise of Judah squarely at the feet of the house of David. The general denunciations of Judah's shepherds have already been noted. Jeremiah specifically denounces the abuses of the Davidic king. The striking thing about these denunciations is the way in which the conduct of the king determines the future of Judah. Jeremiah 21:11–12 urges the king to further civil righteousness to avoid the wrath of God upon the nation. Jeremiah 22:1–5 makes the execution of civil justice and the protection of the poor from oppression by the king the determining factor in whether Judah will experience the blessing or the curse (also Jer 22:13f). Second Kings 23:26–27 relates the ultimate destruction of the city and the temple immediately to the abuses of Manasseh, the king. The account of Manasseh's reign in 2 Kings 21 shows that it was both his idolatry (vv. 2–8) and his violence or civil injustice (v. 16) that provoked Yahveh.

The house of David reached the pinnacle of its power, glory, and extent in the reign of Solomon. Solomon's sins were already in the latter part of his reign, laying the foundation for the decline of the fortunes of the Davidic kings. Psalm 89, written during the reign of Rehoboam,[24] attests that believing Israel was shocked by the swift, sudden, and severe character of the divine chastening that fell on the Davidic line. Rehoboam's folly, the consequent loss of the ten northern tribes, the invasion of Shishak, the plundering of Judah and the temple all foreshadow the ultimate demise of Judah. Even the reason given by Yahveh for Shishak's success reminds one of the final destruction of the theocracy and the exile: "But they will become his slaves so that they may learn the difference between My service and the service of the kingdoms of the countries" (2 Chr 12:8).

The remaining history of Judah is the story of continued political and religious decline. New low points are reached first in the royal alliance with the house of Ahab and then in the shattering abuses of Manasseh. Occasional glimmers of the original Davidic glory are seen in the preservation of Joash, the deliverance of Hezekiah, and the renewal under Josiah before the light of David vanishes in the exile.

The account of the last four Davidic kings reverberates with the reversal of the Davidic blessings. Each king does evil in the sight of Yahveh (2 Kgs 23:32, 37; 24:9, 19). Each is taken from Jerusalem to the humiliation of exile (2 Kgs 23:34; 24:15; 25:7; 2 Chr 36:6). The temple is plundered twice before its ultimate destruction (2 Chr 36:7, 10, 18). At least three deportations depopulate the land and the city of Jerusalem (2 Kgs 24:10–16; 25:11–12; Dan. 1:7).

C. The Restoration of the Theocracy

Taking up the subject of the restoration of the theocracy, one confronts one of the most crucial and yet most complex of Old Testament issues. An illustration of this complexity may be seen in the contrasting notes on which the accounts of the destruction

---

24 This is the position of commentators as diverse as Delitzsch, J. A. Alexander, and Gleason Archer in Gleason Leonard Archer, *A Survey of Old Testament Introduction* (Chicago: Moody, 2007).

of the theocracy (2 Kgs 25; 2 Chr 36) conclude. Both allude to the promises of the Davidic covenant. Yet what a difference there is! Second Kings 25:27–30 records the "lifting up of Jehoiachin's head" by Evil-Merodach. The implication is certainly clear. It is, as several commentators see, that God has yet mercy and exaltation in store for David's house.[25]

The approach of 2 Chronicles 36:22–23 is distinctly different. The allusion is still to the Davidic covenant, but now, however, it is not a son of David but Cyrus, king of Persia, who gains a quasi-Davidic status. He fulfills the function of the son of David whom God appoints to build His house (cf. 2 Sam 7:13; 1 Chr 17:12; 22:10; 28:6, 10, 20; 29:19; 2 Chr 6:2 with 2 Chr 36:23; Ezra 1:2). This unusual status of Cyrus will be enlarged upon later. The point here is that these differing perspectives alert us to the complexity of the subject about to be addressed.

The higher-critical tradition finds in such differing perspectives conflicting theologies. It finds in the disappointments of the Medo-Persian restoration the historical frustration and nullification of the hopes created by Jeremiah, Ezekiel, and others. While a thorough rebuttal of this tradition is neither possible nor appropriate here, the conviction may be expressed that such an approach inevitably misses both the richness and the real intent of the Scripture. Further, by implicitly denying the validity of the Christological interpretation of the Old Testament, it denies one of the oldest and most fundamental of the tenets of Christianity itself and thereby becomes non-Christian.[26]

The denial of the higher-critical oversimplification of the issues entails an eschatological interpretation of the restoration of the theocracy. It thus raises the important but difficult issue of the proper understanding of the Old Testament eschatological statements. Nothing like a thorough treatment is possible

---

25　See C. F. Keil and Robert Jamieson in Archer, *A Survey of Old Testament Introduction*.

26　J. N. D. Kelly, *Early Christian Doctrines* (New York: Harper and Row, 1978), 32.

here. Yet a certain approach will be briefly defended. It is to be noted that the subject at hand provides an excellent paradigm for understanding and takes us to the heart of biblical eschatology.

1. The Medo-Persian Restoration

The mixed reaction to the laying of the foundation of the temple after the exile (Ezra 38:13; Hag 2:1–3) epitomizes the dual perspective with which the Old Testament presents the Medo-Persian restoration. It may be presented both as the restoration of the theocracy (in a limited sense) and as the continuation of the exilic bondage (in the deepest sense).

A superficial reading of Jeremiah might lead one to the opinion that the seventy-year exile would issue in the full restoration of the theocratic kingdom. The prophecy of the seventy years (Jer 25, 29) occurs in the general context of Messianic prophecies (Jer. 23, 31–33). There are other reasons for seeing a theocratic restoration motif in the Medo-Persian restoration. The restoration to the land, the temple with its precious articles (Ezra 1:5–11; 5:1–6, Neh 12:28–39), the civil order enforced by civil penalties (Ezra 7:25–26), and all of this under the reign of "God's anointed," the quasi-Davidic Cyrus and the actual leadership of Zerubbabel, a son of David (1 Chr 3:19; Matt 1:12) points to this motif.

But whatever degree of theocratic restoration took place, it was a far cry from even the last and lowest days of pre-exilic Judah (Ezra 3:8–13), not to mention the golden age of Solomon. However Cyrus and Zerubbabel typified the Davidic messiah, Cyrus was not a son of David, and Zerubbabel not a king (Jer 23:5; 30:9; 33:14–26; Ezek 34:23–24; 37:24–25).

This brings us directly to the second motif: the Medo-Persian restoration as the continuation of the exilic bondage. This is—in the end—the deepest insight of the Old Testament presentation.

No Davidic king returns to reign in Jerusalem. With this fact, one may directly connect the explicit statements of Ezra and

Nehemiah. In his prayer of confession over the mixed marriages, Ezra mentions the captivity of Judah's kings as well as the rest of Judah. He then says,

> But now for a brief moment grace has been shown from the LORD our God, to leave us an escaped remnant and to give us a peg in His holy place, that our God may enlighten our eyes and grant us a little reviving in our bondage. For we are slaves; yet in our bondage, our God has not forsaken us, but has extended loving-kindness to us in the sight of the kings of Persia, to give us reviving to raise up the house of our God, to restore its ruins, and to give us a wall in Judah and Jerusalem. (Ezra 9:8–9)

Nehemiah 9:36–37 contains similar sentiments:

> Behold, we are slaves today, and as to the land which You gave to our fathers to eat of its fruit and its bounty, behold, we are slaves in it. Its abundant produce is for the kings whom You have set over us because of our sins; they also rule over our bodies and over our cattle as they please, so we are in great distress.

The thought (Deut 28:33, 48) and the very language ("distress" [Deut 31:17, 21] and "slaves" and "bondage," both derived from *ebed* [Deut 28:68]) characterize the situation of the returned remnant as a continuation of the exilic situation. More than that, the repeated use of *ebed* or its derivatives characterizes the situation as like that of the bondage preceding the Exodus (Exod 13:3, 14; 20:2; Deut 5:6, 15, 6:12, 21; 7:8; 8:14, 13:5; 15:15; 16:12; 24:18, 22). The mention of the heathen kings implies that slavery and bondage are their lot because Persian kings rule them, not a son of David.

Other elements of Ezra-Nehemiah underscore this motif: the repeated emphasis on the sin of the returned remnant (Ezra

9:1–10:44; Neh 5:1–13; 13:1–31), discouragement in the building of the temple (Hag 1:5), fierce and sometimes effective opposition that delays the construction of the temple and the wall (Ezra 4:1–24; 5:3–6:15; Neh 1:3; 2:9, 10; 4:1–23; 6:1–14), and the failure of many Jews even to desire to return (Ezra 8:15–20).

2. The Eschatological Restoration

These conditions fell far short of the conditions prophesied by Jeremiah and Ezekiel. They foretold the triumphant reign of a Davidic king over a purified, multiplied, secure, and obedient people in a restored, theocratic civil order in the land (Jer 23:3–7; 31:27–37; 32:37–44; 33:1–26; Ezek 11:14–21; 20:33–44; 34:11–31; 36:22–38; 37:24–38). These are the most common features. Other features that transcend the Medo-Persian restoration include Ezekiel's wondrous temple (Ezek 40–48), the reunion of Israel and Judah (pointing to the reversal of the first historical act of judgment on the Davidic dynasty (Ezek 37:15–23; Jer 3:18; 31:1–31), and the universalizing of the theocracy in a way that transcends the old order (Jer 3:16–17; cf. Zech 6:11–14; 14:9–21).

The response of faith to the Medo-Persian restoration is not to question such promises. Rather, it sees in this restoration the typical and germinate fulfillment of promises that receive their ultimate fulfillment in the eschaton.[27] Indications were not lacking, however, before the Medo-Persian restoration that these promises would not be its immediate issue. Cyrus, the restorer, was not to be a Davidic king (Isa 45:4; 46:11; Jer 25:14). It is, however, in the prophecies of Daniel that it is clearly taught that the end of the seventy years would not see the restoration of the theocratic kingdom. Indeed, seventy sevens would pass in the circumstances of partial restoration before the appearance of Messiah, the Prince (Dan 9:25).

It is the subject of the theocratic kingdom along with its disruption that form the controlling backdrop of the prophecies of

---

27   Fairbairn, *The Typology of Scripture*, 1:126f

Daniel (Dan 1:1–7; 9:1–27). This is well-known, but its pervasive significance is not generally appreciated. This is particularly true of the foundational visions of Daniel 2 and 7. Why are just these four kingdoms chosen? What is so special about them? Why aren't the earlier Egyptian and Assyrian empires the subject of like prophecy? Is it their extent that controls their selection?[28] It is rather the theocratic disruption that provides the rationale for these prophecies. They begin with Nebuchadnezzar's Babylon and span Medo-Persia, Greece, and Rome because these empires were those to bear rule over the people of God during the theocratic disruption.[29] They retain this authority until the restoration of the theocracy (Dan 2:34–35, 44; 7:23–27). One of the main purposes of these visions was to warn the people of God that not merely the Babylonians but three additional Gentile kingdoms would bear rule over them before this restoration. Their message is, thus, analogous to that of Daniel 9:24f. It is that not merely seventy years but seventy sevens must transpire before the Davidic reign returns. Fairbairn perceives this relation:

> Not only so; but when the kingdom had fallen to its very foundations, and to the eye of sense lay smitten by the rod of Babylon as with an irrecoverable doom, that precisely was the time, and Babylon itself the place, chosen by God to reveal, through his servant Daniel, the certain resurrection of the kingdom, and its ultimate triumph over all rival powers and adverse influences. In contradistinction to the Chaldean and other worldly kingdoms, which were all destined to pass away, and become like the dust of the summer threshing-floor, he announced the setting up of a kingdom by the God of heaven, which should never

---

28   Leon Wood, *A Commentary on Daniel* (Grand Rapids: Zondervan, 1976), 182.

29   With the majority of conservative interpreters, this treatment assumes that the four kingdoms of Daniel are to be identified with the successive empires of Babylon, Medo-Persia, Greece, and Rome. Cf. Wood, Baldwin, Young, Leupold.

> be destroyed—a kingdom which, in principle, should be the same with the Jewish theocracy and in history should form but a renewal and prolongation, in happier circumstances, of its existence; for it was to be, as of old, a kingdom of priests to God, or of the people of the saints of the Most High; and as such, an everlasting kingdom, which all the dominions were to serve and obey.[30]

The period of the Gentile kingdoms is, then, the period of the theocratic disruption. The special thing about these kingdoms is not their geographical extent but the fact that they bear rule over the people of God in the interim between the disruption and restoration of the theocratic kingdom. They replace the theocratic government during this interim.

All this raises the question of the character and timing of the restoration of the theocratic kingdom. This is all the more necessary if we are to assess the significance of all this for the church. If the theocratic disruption continues today, the church's relationship to civil government will be governed by the principles that governed Israel subsequent to the exile. If one holds that the theocratic kingdom has now been restored, then the relation of post-exilic Israel to civil authority has very little to do with the church and the present era of redemptive history. A dispensational approach to the theocratic kingdom that severs the church and Israel will have the same result.

Among evangelical and conservative interpreters of Daniel, a sharp cleavage exists on the timing of the coming of the kingdom prophesied in Daniel 2 and 7. In general, it is fair to say that dispensational, premillennial interpreters hold to a future restoration of that kingdom associated with the second coming of Christ. The idea of a revived Roman empire is normally associated with this view.[31] Anti-Chiliasts and some premillennialists have held that

---

30   Fairbairn, *The Typology of Scripture*, 2:439–440.
31   Wood, *A Commentary on Daniel*, 72f.

the kingdom of God promised in chapters 2 and 7 came in the events associated with Christ's first advent.[32]

A growing number of evangelical scholars are committed to what might be called a synthesis of these views at least regarding their view of the coming of the kingdom.[33] These scholars recognize a tension in the New Testament regarding the coming of the kingdom: an "already" and a "not yet" in the coming of the kingdom. They believe the kingdom prophesied in the Old Testament unfolds itself in two successive stages. The kingdom foretold by the prophets without self-conscious distinction between these two phases (1 Pet 1:10–11) comes indeed, but first in an inaugural and then in a consummate form. This is perhaps the unique feature of New Testament eschatology and pervades its thought structures (see, e.g., 1 Cor 15:20–28).

It is, however, in Matthew, the "Jewish" gospel, the gospel of the son of David, in which *basileia* (kingdom) occurs fifty-five times and *basileus* (king) twenty-three times, that this doctrine gets its clearest exhibition. It is precisely from Matthew one would expect the clearest teaching on the restoration of the theocratic kingdom.

The teaching of Matthew on the restoration of the theocratic kingdom comes to its classic expression in the parables of Matthew 13. These have for their peculiar purpose the warning, instruction, and encouragement of the disciples concerning the nature of the coming of the kingdom. These parables have for their backdrop Jesus's clear assertion that the kingdom had come (Matt 12:28).[34] The excitement and enthusiasm created by this mighty proclamation would, however, soon begin to wane in the absence of all-transforming works of God in judgment and grace

---

32 Fairbairn, *The Typology of Scripture*, 2:440f.

33 Cf. G. E. Ladd, *A Theology of the New Testament* (Grand Rapids: Eerdmans, 1974); Herman Ridderbos, *The Coming of the Kingdom*, trans. by H. de Jongste (Philadelphia: Presbyterian & Reformed, 1962); Anthony Hoekema, *The Bible and the Future* (Grand Rapids: Eerdmans, 1979); Geerhardus Vos, *Pauline Eschatology* (Grand Rapids: Eerdmans, 1972).

34 Ridderbos, *The Coming of the Kingdom*, 40–41.

that the Jews regarded as synonymous with the coming of the kingdom. These expectations can be epitomized no better than in the preaching of the last and greatest of the prophets, John the Baptist:

> And the axe is already laid at the root of the trees; every tree therefore that does not bear good fruit is cut down and thrown into the fire. As for me, I baptize you in water for repentance, but He who is coming after me is mightier than I, and I am not even fit to remove His sandals; He Himself will baptize you with the Holy Spirit and fire. And His winnowing fork is in His hand and He will thoroughly clean his threshing floor: and He will gather His wheat into the barn, but He will burn up the chaff with unquenchable fire. (Matt 3:10–12)

The note of impending and universal judgment is patent in John's proclamation. Such expectations set the Jewish followers of Christ up for confusion, doubt, and stumbling because of the delay of such a sweeping transformation after the proclamation that the kingdom had come. Again, John the Baptist epitomizes these dangers. Not, of course, that his prophecy was wrong, but rather that like the Old Testament prophets (1 Pet 1:10–11), he was not totally aware of the significance of his own prophecies. A humble Jesus and rotting in prison were not John's idea of the kingdom of God. His early confidence (John 1:29f.; Matt 3:13f.) wavers, and he asks, "Are You the Expected One, or shall we look for someone else?" (Matt 11:3). Jesus's reply cites His miraculous signs and concludes, "Blessed is he who does not take offense at Me" (v. 6). It is the confusion John has just displayed that warrants the words of Jesus, "Truly, I say to you, among those born of women there has not arisen anyone greater than John the Baptist; Yet he who is least in the kingdom of heaven is greater than he" (v. 11). Greater, Jesus means, precisely in the point of his understanding of the coming of the kingdom. It is as to insight into the nature of the kingdom era—which insight was the peculiar glory of the prophets—that he who is least in the kingdom is greater than John the Baptist, the last and greatest of the prophets.

The parables of Matthew 13, then, are Jesus's explanation to His disciples of the mysteries of the kingdom so that they will not be stumbled by the character of His person and ministry. It is not possible to provide an in-depth analysis of these parables here. The studies of Ladd and Ridderbos provide such an analysis and support the view advocated here.[35] The following survey sufficiently illuminates their thrust for the purpose at hand.

The common emphasis of these parables is that the kingdom of God has come and is present but that this is inseparably related to a further future, glorious, and consummate coming of the kingdom. Each of these parables picks up this common emphasis and elaborates it in its own peculiar fashion.

The parable of the four soils emphasizes that the kingdom is present in the sowing of the Word of God. This emphasis is elaborated in two directions. First, the presence of the kingdom is consistent with the rejection of the Word and its consequent fruitlessness in the lives of some who hear it. If the kingdom is present as the sowing of seed, such fruitlessness is to be expected. Second, the presence of the kingdom is vindicated by the amazing fruitfulness of the Word in those who truly receive it.

The parable of the tares elaborates what was implicit in the first parable. The kingdom of God comes in two stages. It will come as the eschatological harvest, but it must for that very reason come first as seed time. Extraordinary as the thought must have been to the Jewish mind, good and evil men will coexist in the world in the time of the kingdom. The coming of the kingdom does not mean the immediate destruction of the wicked. The Messiah comes first as sower and then as harvester. It is not His will that the wicked be immediately destroyed.

---

35 Ridderbos, *The Coming of the Kingdom*, 121–147. See also Ladd, *A Theology of the New Testament*, 93–101.

The point of the parable of the dragnet is almost, if not completely, synonymous with that of the tares. Not only in agriculture but also in fishing, two distinct phases occur. First, there is gathering, then there is sorting. Until the time of separation, good and bad coexist together.

The twin parables of the treasure and the pearl have related emphases. First, Jesus intimates that the kingdom is present in a hidden and unexpected form. Second, Jesus declares that in order to possess the kingdom, there will be the need of total sacrifice. To a Jew with ideas of a glorious, earthly kingdom, possessing the kingdom meant glory, riches, fame, and honor. Jesus says a flat no to that idea regarding the nature of the inaugural kingdom. Possessing the kingdom would rather mean the total sacrifice of this world's possessions that the true riches of the kingdom may be attained hereafter.

The parables of the mustard seed and leaven are also similar in emphasis. The main emphasis of these parables is again that the kingdom comes in two phases. More especially, Jesus is affirming that the present, apparent insignificance of Himself and His followers is no bar to their being the present manifestation of that kingdom that would one day attain supreme dominion. Jesus's answer is first the seed, then the tree. First the absurdly small bit of leaven in over a bushel of meal, and then the whole leavened.

Applying this framework to the interpretation of Daniel and the restoration of the theocratic kingdom, one obtains the result that a tension exists between the "already" and "not yet" aspects of the restoration of the theocratic kingdom.

It is possible to construct an impressive argument for the present restoration of the theocratic kingdom from the New Testament. The motifs of the Davidic covenant find affirmation in many different ways in the New Testament. David's Son has now been exalted and exercises all authority in heaven and on earth (Matt 28:18–20; Eph 1:20–22; Acts 2:34–36; Rom 1:3–4). He reigns in Jerusalem (Gal 4:26; Heb 12:22–24). There He occupies David's throne (Acts 2:30–31). There is the full unification of the throne of God and of David. He occupies the throne of God Himself (Rev 3:21; 5:1–13) in the temple of God (Heb 8:1–6).

Yet all this finds its focal point in heaven (Phil 3:20; Gal 4:26; Heb 12:22f). As to this world, the New Testament insists "we do not yet see all things subjected to him" (Heb 2:8f.; 1 Cor 15:20–28). Premillennialists have been right, therefore, to insist on a future, earthly reign. The meek will inherit and reign upon the earth (Matt 5:5; Rev 5:9, 10). The restoration of the theocratic kingdom means security under the Davidic king for the people of God (Jer 23:5–6; 33:14–18; Ezek 34:20–25; 37:24–28). This is by no means the lot of the people of God in the present, evil age (2 Tim 3:12; Acts 14:22). Thus, while we may speak of the heavenly and spiritual inauguration of the theocratic kingdom, we must never forget that its earthly manifestation is crucial and is yet to come. This the older anti-Chiliast writers tended to miss or neglect.[36]

When one is speaking of civil authority, however, one is speaking of a very earthly and external issue. It is, then, the perspective of the "not yet" that is regulative in relation to the subject of whether our civil allegiance belongs to the Gentile kingdoms or the inaugural theocratic kingdom. As to earthly, civil authority, the theocratic kingdom is not yet. The eschatological regathering of (new) Israel awaits (Matt 8:11–12; 24:29–31; Luke 13:29). The "times of the Gentiles" continue until the end of the age.[37] The

---

36 Fairbairn, *The Typology of Scripture*, 2:441.
37 *Understanding the Times*, ed. by William Culbertson (Grand Rapids: Zondervan, 1965), 17, 116, 121, 122, 161–163. Norval Geldenhuys, *Commentary on the Gospel of Luke* (Grand Rapids: Eerdmans, 1975), 528, 529, 536. These references, the first by a dispensationalist, the second by an amillennialist, illustrate the spectrum of eschatological opinion that agrees in identifying the times of the Gentiles with the period of the four Gentile kingdoms of Daniel, the period of the disruption of the theocratic kingdom. Exegetical facts that encourage this identification are the allusions to Daniel in the surrounding context of this phrase, Luke 21:20 and 27, and the linguistic parallels between the use of *kairoi* here and its frequent use in Daniel with reference

new Jerusalem in its earthly manifestation is not yet (Rev 21:1–7). Jesus, Paul, and Peter command submission to Daniel's fourth kingdom (Matt 22:15f.; Rom 13:1f.; 1 Pet 2:13f.).[38] Jesus refuses the offer of a position of civil authority in the days of his flesh (Luke 12:13–14; John 6:15).

We are now in a position, therefore, to assess the significance for the church of post-exilic Israel's relation to the Gentile civil authorities. The conclusion must be that the church finds itself in a continuation of the "times of the Gentiles" and that for this reason, the Christian's duty to the Gentile kingdom is similar and even identical to that of post-exilic Israel. A study of the authority of the Gentile kingdoms over the people of God is, therefore, relevant for and applicable to the Christian.[39]

---

to the Gentile kingdoms. See especially Dan 2:21; 7:25; 9:26–27. The plural may have for its significance a reference to the plurality of Gentile kingdoms, Daniel 2 and 7. The similarity with Rom 11:25 is superficial and deceptive. This is clear from the fact that the fullness of the Gentiles is not a reference to a period of time, while "times of the Gentiles" is.

38 It is the writer's conviction that the Roman Empire is the fourth kingdom of Daniel, but this is, of course, a matter of intense debate among Daniel scholars. For the purposes at hand, it is not crucial that this identification be maintained. Though the identification of Rome as the fourth kingdom gives an added poignancy to the New Testament requirement of subordination to the Roman civil authority, the alternative interpretation (which identifies the fourth kingdom with that of Antiochus Epiphanes) leaves the basic significance of the four kingdoms the same. They symbolize or epitomize all the Gentile kingdoms that will bear rule over the people of God during the disruption of the theocratic kingdom until the return of Christ.

39 The interpretive framework adopted in this treatment sees Dan 2 and 7 fulfilled in the two-stage unfolding of the kingdom. It holds that it was literally "in the days of those kings" that the God of heaven restored the theocratic kingdom. It is not forced with the futurist to adopt the questionable expedients of a "revived Roman empire," a "gap," a "postponed kingdom," or an unprophesied "parenthesis." On the other hand, it is not forced with the preterist to find the complete fulfillment of the theocratic kingdom in the church as it now exists. In the second stage of its unfolding these prophecies find their visible and earthly fulfillment.

THE CIVIL AUTHORITIES OF THE PEOPLE OF GOD

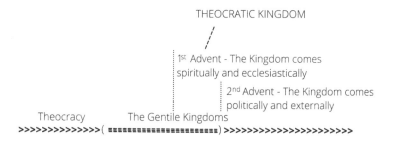

II. The Authority of the Gentile Kingdoms

The discussion thus far has acquainted us with the disruption of the theocratic kingdom and the ascendancy of the Gentile kingdoms over the people of God. The fact, however, that in God's sovereign or decretive will the Gentiles have achieved power over the people of God does not itself solve the issue of whether this

---

It is appropriate to remark that the idea of a two-phase fulfillment must apply not only to the theocratic kingdom but also to the fourth kingdom of Daniel's vision. Just as "the coming of the son of man" (Dan 7:13–14) unfolds itself in the two events of Christ's ascension and parousia, even so the fourth and most terrible Gentile kingdom unfolds in two historical manifestations. It is not necessary to suppose that this implies a "revived Roman empire." In the same way, seeing Antiochus Epiphanes and the Roman Caesars as types of the eschatological antichrist does not require us to believe that the antichrist will be Nero Redivivus, etc. What is required is the idea of a universal, civil authority that abuses its God-given authority in systematic persecution of the people of God.

power is to be regarded as legitimate or valid civil authority. Nothing resists God's decretive will (Rom 9:16–20). Nothing escapes God's decretive purpose (Eph 1:11; Rom 9:16–20). "If a calamity occurs in a city has not the LORD done it?" (Amos 3:6). Thus, the mere fact that in God's decree the Gentiles have gained power over Israel does not make legitimate that power. Otherwise, we should have to denounce the saviors whom God sent Israel in the period of Judges. The question is this: Is it not only God's decretive will but also God's preceptive will that the Gentile kingdoms reign over the people of God?

This is related to the broader question of the nature of civil government in general. In a well-known work, Oscar Cullmann has defended the thesis that "the powers" of Romans 13:1 include angelic-demonic powers.[40] The basic question is this: Is civil government, the authority of the Gentile kingdoms, divine or demonic? Is Romans 13 or Revelation 13 the "*classicus locus*" on the subject of civil government?

Interestingly enough, the first and last chapters of the Aramaic portion of Daniel, chapters 2 and 7, confront us immediately with this issue. For, in the opinion of the present writer, the symbolism of Daniel 2 and 7 presents us with two strikingly different views of the Gentile kingdoms. The difference is all the more striking because of the marked similarities of the two visions. The single, great statue in human form in chapter 2 contrasts vividly with the four ferocious beasts of chapter 7. Chapter 2 sets before us via its imagery the Gentile kingdoms as human and exercising a divinely delegated authority. Human form has a positive significance in Daniel (Dan 7:4, 13). There is no hint of the idolatrous in the statue.[41] While the imagery does not hint as to the origin of this statue, verse 37 makes clear the divine right of Nebuchadnezzar's

---

40   Oscar Cullmann, *The State in the New Testament* (New York: Charles Scribner's Sons, 1956), 51f.

41   E. J. Young, *The Prophecy of Daniel* (Grand Rapids: Eerdmans, 1949), 71. See also C. F. Keil, *The Book of Daniel* (Grand Rapids: Eerdmans, 1975), 102.

kingdom (see the discussion of this text below). Many commentators note the unity of the statue in opposition to the diversity of the beasts.[42] This unity points to the fact that a single authority is retained by each of the Gentile kingdoms. The ultimate destruction of the statue may hint at the eventual abuse of its authority but does not indicate that its authority was not God-given. One may compare Psalm 82. In verse 8 of that psalm, God is urged to reclaim the authority He has delegated to the "gods" (civil authorities) because of their abuse of it (vv. 2–7), and judge all the nations. Daniel's calmness and confidence in chapter 2 vividly contrasts with his reaction to the vision of chapter 7. This also points to the idea that the two chapters present the Gentile kingdoms in contrasting ways. It is human civil authority as divinely constituted that the vision of chapter 2 contemplates.

Chapter 7, on the other hand, is filled with the distress and alarm and consternation that fills Daniel's heart in response to its imagery (vv. 7, 15, 28). It is the bestiality of the Gentile kingdoms under demonic control that evoke this response (vv. 3–8, 11). Now it is the abuse of civil authority with its consequent persecution of the people of God that is in view. Of persecution, there was nothing in chapter 2. Now it is prominent (vv. 8, 11, 18–25). It is now not the unity of these kingdoms as possessing a single God-given authority presented but their diversity in their mutual antagonism (7:8, 20, 24; 8:5–8). These beasts originate not by God's preceptive will (2:37) but by the action of God's general providence on the chaotic sea of fallen mankind (7:2–3).[43]

The juxtaposition of these two views of the Gentile kingdoms in Daniel permits two preliminary remarks before we develop them respectively via the post-exilic literature. One may first remark that

---

42 Young, *The Prophecy of Daniel*, 76; Keil, *The Book of Daniel*, 102f.

43 Young, *The Prophecy of Daniel*, 142. Keil, *The Book of Daniel*, 222f. Several commentators notice the contrasting imagery of Dan 2 and Dan 7. Compare Wood, *A Commentary on Daniel*, 178 and Leupold, *Exposition of Daniel* (Minneapolis: Augsburg, 1961), 277 for their interpretations.

the juxtaposition of these two views by Daniel at the beginning and end of Daniel's Aramaic section reminds us that no dichotomy should be erected between the view of the earthly kingdom given in Revelation 13 and that given in Romans 13. Daniel saw nothing inconsistent in these two views. Tension there may be, inconsistency never! The task of biblical scholarship is to penetrate their inner unity and appropriately apply the rich diversity of the biblical presentation. This leads to the second remark. One task that may not be neglected in a study of the biblical view of the state is the penetration of the inner unity of this tension and the assessment of its significance for the biblical view of the origin and nature of the state.

A. The Authority of the Gentile Kingdoms as Divine

Do the Gentile kingdoms possess a legitimate civil authority over the people of God? Is their power *de jure* as well as *de facto*? In the course of our examination of this subject, we shall note in order the validity, responsibility, and perpetuity of their authority. The first is our major concern with the second and third topics dependent on and subordinate to its development.

1. Its Validity

Here we shall examine the varied contributory evidence of the post-exilic literature by looking first at the validity of Nebuchadnezzar's rule and then at that of Cyrus's rule. The reasons for this development will be evident when the perpetuity of Gentile authority is developed. For the present we are assuming that the authority of these two kings descends to their respective successors.

a. Nebuchadnezzar

So various are the motifs that establish the divine legitimacy of Nebuchadnezzar's rule over the people of God that one might be tempted to speak of a pro-Babylonian polemic in the relevant literature, but compare Jeremiah 50–51 and Daniel 5.

Daniel 2:37 asserts, "You, O king, are the king of kings, to whom the God of heaven has given the kingdom, the power, the strength, and the glory." This text was mentioned above briefly and must now be developed with regard to its assertion of the legitimacy of Nebuchadnezzar's rule. Several corroboratory remarks will make this clear. The terms *kingdom*, *power*, *strength*, and *glory* imply the idea that not mere power but actual authority has been divinely granted to Nebuchadnezzar.[44] (Note the frequent repetition of this theme in Dan 4:36–37; 5:18–19). The parallel use of this terminology in Daniel 7:14, 22, 27 of the kingdom of God also suggests this point. Also relevant is the allusion in Daniel 2:37 to Psalm 8:6–8 and through it to Genesis 1:26–27 noticed by several of the commentators.[45] This ties Nebuchadnezzar's rule to the image of God and thereby establishes its validity.

This allusion to Psalm 8:6–8 is also present in Jeremiah's classic statement of Nebuchadnezzar's authority in chapters 27 and 28 (see especially 27:5–6; 28:14). Other indications of his legitimate, civil authority in those chapters include the naming of Nebuchadnezzar as God's servant (27:6), the threat to punish severely any nation that does not submit to his yoke (27:8), the promise to preserve the nation that does submit (27:11), and the application of all this to Zedekiah and Judah (27:12–15). The death of the false prophets who prophesied against Babylon—some at the hand of Nebuchadnezzar—underscores the whole (Jer 28:1–17; 29:21–23).

Related to all this is the emphasis of 2 Chronicles 36 and Ezekiel 17 that Zedekiah, in rebelling against Nebuchadnezzar, had broken solemn covenant not only with Nebuchadnezzar but with God (2 Chr 36:13; Ezek 17:11–21; Ezra 4:19).

These motifs enable us to understand the basis on which Jeremiah issued the unprecedented call to fall away or apostatize to the king of Babylon, promising life to those who did (Jer 21:8–10; 37:13–15; 38:1–28). This recommendation contrasts starkly with

44 See Brown, Driver, Briggs, *Hebrew and English Lexicon of the Old Testament* (Oxford: Clarendon, 1962).

45 Young, *The Prophecy of Daniel*, 73. See also Joyce Baldwin, *Daniel* (Downers Grove: IL: Intervarsity Press, 1978), 93.

the divine prohibition against going to Egypt (Jer 42:7; 37:3–10; Ezek 32).

This call to fall away is followed up with the advice of Jeremiah 29:1–7. The Jews are to pray for and seek the welfare of the city where they are exiled. This the exiled Jews did zealously, as the example of Daniel and his three friends proves. Jews rose to positions of prominence in the exile.[46] Daniel refused the king's food but not his service (Dan 1:8–21), rising to the pinnacle of civil authority along with his friends (2:46–49), indicating genuine loyalty to the king (4:19), and finding this loyalty reciprocated (6:14–24).

The kindness of the Babylonian kings to the Jews, in fact, is a prominent theme in the literature. Evil-Merodach favors Jehoiachin (2 Kgs 25:27–30), just as Nebuchadnezzar had kindly treated Jeremiah (Jer 39:11–40:6). This kindness is all the more striking because of the way it contrasts with the harsh treatment and imprisonment of Jeremiah by Zedekiah (Jer 37:11–38:28; Ezra 9:9).

The giving of divine revelation to one outside the covenant is uncommon enough that this may also be a further indication of the almost "pro-Babylonian polemic" (Daniel 2 and 4). Certainly Nebuchadnezzar's response recorded in Daniel 4 to the second vision and his chastisement should be seen as supporting the legitimacy of his authority (Dan 3:24–30).

b. Cyrus

Many of these motifs recur with reference to Cyrus and the Medo-Persian kings. The acknowledgment of the Most High God is, if anything, more prominent (2 Chr 36:22–23; Ezra 1:2–4; 6:10–12; 7:11–12, 19–26; Dan 6:25–28). Too much, of course, must not be made out of such acknowledgments, but their prominence in the literature should convince us that the writers regarded them as more than stylized and insincere formulas. The fact that the

---

46   "Life in the Diaspora," *Biblical Archeologist*, XXXVII (1974), 1.

Jews loyally served the Persian kings is also pervasively recorded. There are Sheshbazzar, Zerubbabel, and Nehemiah, the governors; Nehemiah, the cupbearer; Mordecai, who revealed a plot on the king's life (Esth 2:21–23) and rose to an exalted position (6:1–14; 8:1–2, 15–17; 9:4; 10:2–3). Thus, those who remained in exile during the Persian period continued to seek the welfare of their cities (Jer. 29:1–7).

Two special marks of authority belong to Cyrus and the Persian kings:

1. They are the appointed instruments of God to rebuild the city and temple, a Davidic function (2 Chr 36:22–23; Ezra 1:2f.; 7:6–11; 6:14). This strongly suggests they possess a civil legitimacy of the same character as the Davidic dynasty.

2. It is undoubtedly this work (Isa 44:26–28; 45:13; 46:11) that gives Cyrus the exalted titles of Yahveh's "shepherd" and "anointed one" (Isa 44:28; 45:1). Such titles strongly suggest the civil legitimacy of Cyrus and his Persian successors.

2. Its Responsibility

If Nebuchadnezzar is Yahveh's servant, and Cyrus His shepherd and anointed one, they are for that very reason to rule for Him and in accord with His will. Failure to do so results in divine judgment (Jer 50–51; Dan 4; 5:17–30). Yahveh requires deep humility before and acknowledgment of the Most High God (Dan 4:37), righteousness and mercy to the poor (Dan. 4:27), keeping sacred that which God regards as holy (Dan 5:1–4), and refraining from persecuting God's people (Dan 7:25–26).

3. Its Perpetuity

By speaking of the perpetuity of their authority, it is meant that the authority given originally to Nebuchadnezzar is passed on to the Gentile kingdoms that rule over the Israel of God until the second advent of Christ. The starting point for this is again the imagery of Daniel 2 noted above. The four Gentile kingdoms (and the number four may have a symbolic significance beyond its literal significance) are seen as one entity. One awesome symbol of civil authority in the hands of man represents them all.

The thought contained in this symbolism is expanded in the literature. It is not merely Nebuchadnezzar but his sons also who will rule (Jer 27:7). It is not only Nebuchadnezzar, the dynastic head of Babylon, who possesses genuine authority. Cyrus also has such authority (see Jer 50:44 where Yahveh asserts His prerogative to appoint a successor to the Babylonian kingdom). Thus, the civil authority of the first two of the four kingdoms is attested. Therefore, the Jews continue to seek the welfare of their exilic cities even after the return of the remnant to Judah and serve the successors of Cyrus (Esth 10:2–3; 2:21–23; Neh 2:1–8).

The apostle Paul utters what is only the logical conclusion of all this in Romans 13:1 when he says, "Let every person be in subjection to the governing authorities. For there is no authority except from God, *and those which exist are established by God.*" The statement is often understood (and is certainly true) in the abstract or general sense, but it is nonetheless the fruit of a rich historical movement. For it was of the Roman Empire, the fourth and iron kingdom of Daniel 2, of which Paul was speaking. The four Gentile kingdoms of Daniel 2 include ultimately all non-theocratic civil authority ruling over the people of God until the end of the age and the dawning of the theocratic kingdom. Nebuchadnezzar's authority becomes that of his sons, and their authority devolves to Cyrus and his successors, and thence to Greece and Rome. Rome's authority unfolds to include all human, civil authority during this age until its eschatological consummation in the kingdom of Antichrist.

B. The Authority of the Gentile Kingdoms as Demonic

The heading that stands over this book could be misunderstood.

The authority of the four Gentile kingdoms is only demonic in a qualified sense. The Gentile kingdoms, as we shall see, embody a bestial (and hence demonic) element from the beginning that comes more and more to characterize them in their eschatological development. This aspect of Gentile power will be examined by looking at its origins, its manifestations, its development, and its corollary.

1. Its Origins

One might foresee the bestiality of the Gentile kingdoms in the mere fact that it is fallen humanity God invests with civil authority. No redemptive provision is granted with this investiture. Hence its abuse was certain.

Another circumstance, however, in the origin of the power of the Gentile kingdoms points more clearly to the negative aspects of their power. Their power rises over the people of God in fulfillment of covenantal curses on the wickedness of Israel (Jer 1:15–16; 2 Kgs 23:6–7; 2 Chr 36:11–17; Deut 28:25, 36, 49f.). With such an origin, one might expect that conditions for the people of God under such rulers would be less than ideal. In fact, one may speak of a curse-character in the rule of the Gentile kingdoms. This is certainly reflected in the attitudes of Ezra and Nehemiah, who liken their condition to that of Israel before the exodus. It is the condition of bondage and slavery under foreign kings (Ezra 9:8–9; Neh 9:36). This language reflects on the fact that it is not one of their countrymen but a foreigner who rules them. Deuteronomy 17:14–20 associates foreign rule with tyrannical and autocratic rule. The glory of the house of David for Israel was that one of their kinsmen ruled them (Ps 89:19; Deut 17:15). Jeremiah 30, in its great promise of restoration, ties the reestablishment of the theocratic kingdom to this thought. One "of them" "out of their midst" will lead and rule God's Israel (v. 21).

THE THEOCRATIC AND GENTILE KINGDOMS

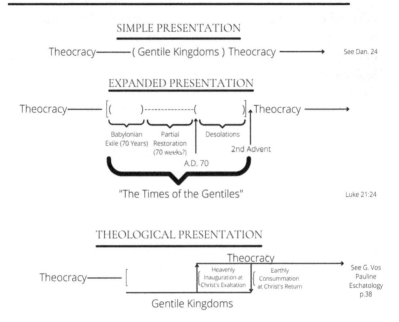

2. Its Manifestations

Various and multiplied instances of the bestiality of the Gentile kingdoms are given in the relevant literature. Daniel, Esther, and to some extent, Ezra contain the most relevant materials.

Daniel, as noted before, portrays the Gentile kingdoms with bestial imagery in chapters 7 and 8. Their power, ferocity, and violence is patent (7:3–8; 8:3–14). It is in connection with these beasts that persecution of the people of God first becomes a subject of Daniel's prophetic visions (Dan 7:21–25; 8:9–14). Daniel 3–6, however, intimate in their historical narratives that systematic persecution could become a reality under the Gentile kings. The common element in the narratives of Daniel 3–6 seems to be the tendency of the Gentile kings to assume divine prerogatives and engage in excessive and idolatrous self-exaltation. This is, by the way, the exact point of which the kings of Israel were to beware

(Deut 17:20). Nothing could make clearer the demonic tendency in these kingdoms.

Chapter 3 reveals the proud, divine pretensions of Nebuchadnezzar in his demand for divine worship. The great statue here stands as the precise antithesis of the deepest demands and highest prerogatives of God in His covenant. The result of Nebuchadnezzar having such pretensions, though not perhaps its self-conscious intention, was the attempted destruction of God's servants. Chapter 4 records the same pride here manifesting itself in the boasting that claims for its own the credit, the honor, and the glory and does not give God His due. Chapter 5 exhibits this same pride as the empty bravado of a doomed king. This bravado leads again to direct conflict with God when it claims the sacred temple vessels for the profanity of its drinking binge. The foolish pretensions of the Gentile kings reach their nadir of degradation and shame in chapter 6. Their divine pretensions are now exhibited in the decree forbidding petitions to "any god or man" and in the repeated refrain that the laws of the kings of the Medo-Persian were divine in their immutability (vv. 8, 12, 15).[47] How despicable is this "god" who by flattery and manipulation is trapped by his own decree, forced to condemn Daniel against his will, and is helpless to save him though he yearns to do so. Thus, chapter 6 provides the *reductio ad absurdum* to the divine pretensions of the Gentile kings. As in chapter 3, however, we are reminded that to live under such bungling gods is a curse often felt by God's Daniels.

Another characteristic that is frequently in view in Daniel is the excessive violence of the Gentile powers. We must, of course, beware of being affected by the sub-biblical sentimentality that pervades modern thought. Kings are given the power of life and death by God Himself (Dan 5:19). Notwithstanding this, the abject fear that the excessive and arbitrary violence of these rulers causes is seen as early in Daniel as 1:10 (Note also 3:6, 19, 22, 6:7, 23, 24).

---

47 Baldwin, *Daniel*, 127. See also W. M. Taylor, *Ruth and Esther* (New York: George H. Doran, 1919), 233.

Esther reinforces the impressions of violent and arbitrary autocratic rule made by Daniel. Esther is terrified even to approach the king unbidden (4:11, 17). Queens are banished (1:13–22), virgins are seized (2:8),[48] high officials are executed (7:7–10), and whole races may be exterminated (3:7–15) at the mere whim of the king. The violence, drunkenness, sensuality, and plots of the Persian court pervade every corner of Esther. Again, and this is at the heart of Esther, the curse and danger of such rule for the people of God is clear (3:1–4:17).

3. Its Development

The demonic character of the Gentile kingdoms unfolds and becomes more prominent in the eschatological development of the Gentile kingdoms. In Daniel 7, it is the fourth and last kingdom that is peculiarly noted for its surpassing strength, terror, and ferocity (v. 7). It is in the later development of this kingdom that the "little horn" exalts himself against God (vv. 8, 11, 20, 25) and destroys the people of God (vv. 21–25). In Daniel 8, it is the third kingdom that is in view. Still, the third kingdom is the last in the context of chapter 8, and it is striking that it exhibits similar developments in its later stages (8:9–14, 23–26). Again, the clear impression is that of the increasing development of the demonic in the Gentile powers.

The New Testament corroborates this. Second Thessalonians 2, in imagery drawn from the latter chapters of Daniel (cf. 2 Thess 2:3–4 with Dan 11:36; 8:10–11; 7:8, 11, 25), speaks of the development of the mystery of lawlessness already at work until its final manifestation (vv. 7f). All this is due to "the activity of Satan" (v. 9). Similarly, in Revelation 12:17, we behold the "dragon" calling up the "beast" from the sea. The whole passage is reminiscent of Daniel's imagery. "The beast" is, of course, the eschatological and worldwide demonic consummation of Gentile power (13:3, 6, 7, 12).

---

48   Taylor, *Ruth and Esther*, 138f.

Daniel and the Bible in general looks for the demonic finally to dominate Gentile power. The bestiality always present will finally issue in "the beast." The tendency to divine pretensions and the danger this poses for the people of God will finally become the systematic assumption of divine prerogatives, the systematic denial of the true God, and the systematic and universal persecution of the people of God.

4. Its Corollary

This paper began with a distinction between the general sovereignty of God and the special kingship administered through His covenants that God sustained with Israel. With the destruction of the theocratic kingdom and the ascendancy of the Gentile kingdoms, an emphasis is given to the idea of God's universal sovereignty over the nations. Repeated, striking statements of divine sovereignty crowd Daniel (Dan 2:19–23, 47; 4:3, 17, 25, 34–35, 37; 6:26–27). Daniel records repeated instances of God's special providence and preservation of his people (Dan 1:9; 3:24–26; 6:19–22; 7:4; 8:25). The message is that God is with His people in the exile. He stands with them in the flames (3:24–26). He sends His angel to shut the lion's mouths (6:19–22).

The same emphasis is everywhere present. Ezekiel is told that God is a sanctuary for His people in their exile (11:14–17). God's name is not mentioned, but God's minute providence is ubiquitous in Esther for the preservation of his people. Cyrus's activities manifest the sovereign purposes and providence of God for His people (Isa 44:24–28; 45:1–7; 45:8–13; 46:8–11). Ezra testifies to God's special providential preservation (7:9–10, 6, 27–28; 8:21–23, 31–32). It is God who "has not forsaken us," he says, "but has extended loving-kindness to us in the sight of the kings of Persia" (9:8–9). Nehemiah also records how God answered prayer and sovereignly disposed the heart of the king (2:1–8). God continued to keep His people (4:15).

Thus, the people of God are helplessly exposed to the ferocity of the Gentile kings but are constantly reminded that God will restrain their bestiality until the restoration of the theocratic kingdom. For the time will come when the saints will possess the kingdom (Dan 7:22).

GENERAL CONCLUSIONS

A. The Commonality of Post-Exilic Israel and the Church in Terms of their Relation to Civil Authority

The data brought forward in this book supports the conclusion that substantial unity and continuity exists between post-exilic Israel and the church on the matter of their relation to the Gentile kingdoms. The church as the New Israel inherits Israel's relation to Gentile authorities and feels their power both in its human and bestial dimensions. C. F. Keil sees the matter clearly: "Accordingly the exile forms a great turning-point in the development of the kingdom of God which He had founded in Israel. With that event the form of the theocracy established at Sinai comes to an end, and then begins the period of the transition to a new form, which was to be established by Christ."[49]

The recognition of the development of a new continuity between Israel and the church at this point in redemptive history must not disguise the remaining discontinuity. Here we must remember the restoration motif noticed in our treatment of the Medo-Persian restoration. There was a typical and partial restoration of the theocracy at that time. While Judah was no longer a kingdom, it was a province of the Persian empire and, thus, a civil entity. Within these limitations, the theocratic civil order continued to be enforced with civil penalties, and the union of church and state remained. The New Testament makes clear that the church is not in continuity with this partially restored theocracy (Matt 21:33–46; Acts 7:1–53 with 6:8–15). This partially restored theocracy dies under divine judgment shortly after the church's establishment.

---

49   Keil, *The Book of Daniel*, 8f.

B. The Non-theocratic Character of Civil Authority until the Return of Christ

The first conclusion reminds us that with the expiration of the partially restored theocratic order, all civil authority ceased to be theocratic as we have defined it in this book. God is no longer the unique king of any civil entity. No nation is now mandated to adhere to a divinely revealed civil order. While the moral principles enshrined in the laws of the old covenant remain authoritative, no nation is bound to the detailed, civil order of Old Testament Israel. Add to all this the destruction of the temple as the earthly throne of Yahveh, and one must also conclude that no longer are church and state a united entity. The redeemed community no longer has a civil structure. Thus, the divine establishment of the Gentile civil authorities means that the separation of the civil and ecclesiastical institutions in human society is now God's preceptive will. The alteration of this order will be signaled only by the return of Christ.

It is pertinent to note that advocacy of the doctrine of just revolution has often been associated with a theocratic view of civil authority. Specifically, it has often been argued that revolution is justified against any state that is not "Christian." Quite obviously, the view of civil authority supported by the foregoing exposition spells destruction to such notions.

C. The Divine Establishment of the Gentile, Civil Authorities

The assertion that no civil authority is now theocratic does not mean, biblically, that civil authority now stands in no relation or only a negative relation to God. The biblical data clearly establishes that the present, Gentile civil authorities are divinely constituted. Clearly, this fact implies the idea that Gentile authorities are responsible to God and owe Him obedience *as civil authorities*. More stress, however, is placed in the literature on the duty of the people of God to subject themselves to the government of these rulers. To resist Nebuchadnezzar was to resist God. The biblical mandate to render obedience to the Gentile kings sheds light on the extent and character of the duty owed to civil authorities. Of course, no obedience was to be rendered to demands that violated the explicit demands of God. On the other hand, service and obedience was to be rendered to uncovenanted, autocratic, proud, idolatrous, abusive, and often bestial rulers. No fact could speak more eloquently the truth that our subjection to civil authority is not conditioned on (our estimate of) the way it is being exercised. Bestial demands and behavior may call for disobedience or flight, but they never provide the grounds for violent resistance or rebellion. If Nebuchadnezzar's self-deifying idolatry and Ahasuerus's tyranny did not give the right of rebellion, then it is hard to imagine any conditions under which the abuse of civil power would warrant rebellion against "the powers that be."

The same fact rebukes the attempt to condition subordination to civil authority on its form. Those who wish to assert that armed rebellion against autocratic or totalitarian regimes is permissible must face the fact that God called His people to subordinate themselves to just such regimes in Babylon and Medo-Persia. What regimes were more autocratic than these?

Yet again, this very fact teaches us that the origin of a civil authority's rule over us does not condition our duty toward it. There are those who suggest that rule originally gained via usurpation or conquest does not possess legitimacy. Such forget it was in just such a way that the Babylonian, Persian, and Roman rule over the people of God originated. Yet the Bible always requires subordination to such authorities.

Worth mentioning here is the fact that examples of rebellions led by Jews against foreign kings during the time of the theocracy are not relevant to the issue now being addressed. Shamgar, Samson, and the other saviors sent to deliver Israel from foreign domination lived before the divine transfer of civil authority to the Gentile kings and before the divine destruction of the theocracy. There is a qualitative redemptive-historical difference between Eglon and Nebuchadnezzar.

D. *The Curse-Character of Life under the Gentile Kingdoms*

The authority of the Gentile kingdoms originated in covenantal curses, and life under them continues and will continue to be a curse to the people of God. The clear prophetic outlook of the Word of God is that the bestial character of these kingdoms will continue to manifest itself and will finally completely dominate the eschatological manifestation of Gentile authority. This is not to be read as permission to ignore or be indifferent to civil righteousness, insofar as it is within our ability to enhance it. Such a conclusion would fly in the face of the totalitarian claims of God and His Word. This conclusion does mean, however, that civil authority is not to be made the object of misdirected hope or consuming attention by the people of God. The mark of the perversion of the biblical perspective is the refocusing of hope on social change. This error pervades modern theologies of social change. The true hope of the people of God is the reestablishment of the theocratic kingdom. This, as the Scripture declares, will be the achievement not of civil reformation but of cataclysmic and supernatural divine intervention.

Chapter 4

DOES ROMANS 13:1–7
FORBID ALL REVOLUTION?
A CRITICAL QUESTION IN
CHRISTIAN POLITICAL THEORY

I. INTRODUCTION

A. *The Importance of the Question*

Does Romans 13:1–7 forbid all revolution?

On the answer to this question hinges the legitimacy of some of our culture's fundamental political assumptions and the consequent baptism of those assumptions into the Christian faith. Though Wayne Boulton has not followed his insights to the conclusions advocated in this book, he has penetratingly stated the challenge posed by Romans 13:1–7 to Christians of our cultural background:

> It always seems to be marching in fresh from the Middle Ages. No biblical passage continues to provoke quite as much controversy in Christian political thought as these verses from the 13th chapter of Paul's letter to the church at Rome. . . . The text is counter-cultural vis-a-vis liberal

115

democracies. It suggests, though it never explicitly states, an antidemocratic theory of power. . . . In the familiar circular logic of democratic theory, we obey government ultimately because government obeys us. When it doesn't, we recognize a right to resist and change it. This conception of government might be called the populist or ascending theory, because power is understood to ascend from the broad base of a pyramid (the people) to its apex (the duke, king, president). Directly opposed to this is the hierocratic or descending theory of political authority and power. Here original power is located in a Supreme Being. . . . Again the metaphorical pyramid appears, but now all original power is located at its apex rather than its base. . . . The descending thesis was dominant in Europe in the Middle Ages; but since the recovery of Aristotle by Thomas Aquinas, and particularly since the Renaissance and the rise of liberal democracies, it has receded into the background. . . . One reason why Romans 13 is controversial today is that it reflects this theory perfectly. In fact, the passage was an essential plank in all Christian versions of the thesis in the Middle Ages. Now that the theory is practically extinct, many Christians wish the text were also! A deep modern objection to Romans 13, in a word, is not religious or theological at all, but cultural. It is a political embarrassment with the stature of Holy Writ.[1]

Does the Bible permit us our liberal, popular-sovereignty, social contract theories of government? The telltale sign of such theories is the right of revolution. If the Word of God forbids revolution, this will entail drastic alterations in our politics.

---

1 Wayne Boulton, "The Riddle of Romans 13," *The Christian Century*, XCIII (1976), 758, 760.

B. *The Background of the Question*

The view that forbids all revolution has often been connected historically with viewpoints that fail to take seriously the claims of the Word and law of God upon the state. Such a failure has been present historically in the anti-revolutionary and pacifistic Anabaptist tradition. In this tradition the state is viewed as *per se* sinful, though used by God to restrain sin. In such a view, the authority of the law of God over the state can scarcely be taken seriously. If the state really conformed to the teaching of Scripture, it would have to cease to exist.[2] Such a failure has also existed in certain (Lutheran and Anglican) circles that have so emphasized the divine right of kings and rulers that their subordination to God and His law have been obscured or even denied in favor of their being regulated by a vague natural law.[3]

The Reformed tradition, on the other hand, has emphasized the sovereignty of God and His law over the state.[4] The subordination of the civil magistrate to God and His law implicit in the designations and functions of civil rulers in Romans 13:1–7 has been emphasized in Reformed exegesis of Romans 13. Most recently, Greg Bahnsen has forcibly presented this emphasis.[5] Early on in the Reformed tradition, this emphasis was, as we have seen previously, associated with the right of revolution against a government that did not sufficiently conform to God's law.[6] This right of revolution has been introduced into Romans 13 through the emphasis of verses 3 and 4 on the restraint of evil and the promotion of good by civil government. This procedure will be examined in section 5.

---

2   John Howard Yoder, *The Politics of Jesus* (Grand Rapids: Eerdmans, 1972), 203–204. In this and his other works, Yoder seeks to mitigate this implication of the Anabaptist tradition but, in our opinion, without success.

3   Yoder, 200.

4   Yoder, 201.

5   Greg L. Bahnsen, *Theonomy in Christian Ethics* (Phillipsburg: Presbyterian and Reformed, 1984), 366_400.

6   Yoder, *The Politics of Jesus*, 201. The work that is classically associated with this emphasis in the Reformed tradition is Samuel Rutherford, *Lex Rex* (Harrisonburg: Sprinkle, 1982).

One of the assumptions of this dissertation, as stated previously, is that the Reformed tradition has been correct in emphasizing that the state is fully subject to the norms of God's Word and is obliged to conform to them. Here, however, is the peculiarity of the teaching of the Word of God and the thesis of this dissertation. While it insists on the subordination of the state to the norms of God and His Word, it denies the deduction that revolution is thereby in some cases justified. This peculiar and distinctive outlook cuts across the grain of the major schools of Christian interpretation, bringing together elements that human wisdom has separated.

C. The State of the Question

Many different theological battles have been fought in the arena of Romans 13:1–7, and in the process, it has been subjected to various contortions and distortions. No one disputes, however, that the basic intention of the text as it stands in Romans is to encourage obedience and subordination (and, thus, not rebellion) toward the Roman civil authorities. This, at any rate, has been too clear to evade. It is not this basic intention that attracts the attention of this paper. It begins with the *ifs*, *ands*, and *buts* appended to this clear intention by commentators. The question addressed here is this: Is *all* revolution forbidden by this passage?

Few of the commentators actually address this question head on. To be sure, many of them state their opinion of the issue but rather as an appendage or assumption not rooted in their treatment of the passage. On the one side, James Moulder regards the issue as so clear that he can simply assume that Romans 13:1–7 forbids all revolution and then move on to the question of whether it prohibits all civil disobedience.[7] Such assumptions are not justified by a survey of recent theological and exegetical opinion of Romans 13:1–7, though they may be by the straightforward clarity of Paul's assertions when properly cleared of modern objections. Such authors as Moulder cites are distinctly in the minority. More

---

7   James Moulder, "Romans 13 and Conscientious Disobedience," *Journal of Theology for Southern Africa*, XXI (December 1977), 13.

common is the opinion expressed by several respectable exegetes that Paul simply does not make clear in Romans 13 what he thought about revolution.[8] Even more common are those who, after giving their understanding of the passage, append the caution that "of course Paul does not mean to forbid all revolution."[9] Cranfield, representative of this class, clearly states that revolution is sometimes necessary and justified. One of a Christian's political responsibilities according to Cranfield is "readiness in certain extreme circumstances to engage in armed rebellion in order to suppress a government that is intolerably unjust and to replace it." Cranfield is careful to tell us, "Here again the New Testament gives us no direct guidance. Neither our Lord's attitude to the Zealots nor Rom. 13:2 settles the matter."[10] Perhaps, however, the most common treatment is that of those who do not distinctly address the issue at all. Such commentators are eager to make the point that Paul's call for obedience is less than universal or unconditional, but they fail to distinguish disobedience and rebellion. Thus, we are left to guess at their attitudes toward rebellion.[11]

---

8   Herman Ridderbos, *Paul*, transl. by John Richard DeWitt (Grand Rapids: Eerdmans, 1975), 324. John Murray, *The Epistle to the Romans* (Grand Rapids: Eerdmans, 1968), 2:150. James L. Garrett, "The Dialectic of Rom. 13:1–7 and Revelation 13: Part One," *The Journal of Church and State*, XVIII (1976), 442.

9   C. E. B. Cranfield, "The Christian's Political Responsibility according to the New Testament," *The Scottish Journal of Theology*, (1962), 188. See also Arland Hultgren, "Reflections on Rom. 13:1–7: Submission to Governing Authorities," XV (1976), 269, dialogue; J. L. C. Abineno, "The State According to Romans Thirteen," *Southeast Asia Journal of Theology*, XIV (1972), 26–27; Marcus Borg, "A New Context for Romans 13," *New Testament Studies*, XIX (January, 1973), 205; Alexander F. C. Webster, "St. Paul's Political Advice to the Haughty Gentile Christians in Rome," *St. Vladimir's Theological Quarterly*, XXV (1981), 260; T. J. Reese, "Pauline Politics: Rom. 13:1–7," *Biblical Theology Bulletin*, III (October, 1973), 333, who may favor this.

10   Cranfield, "The Christian's Political Responsibility," 188.

11   See Hultgren, "Reflections on Rom. 13:1–7," 269; Abineno, "The State According to Romans Thirteen," 26–27; Borg, "A New Context for Romans 13," 205; Webster, "St. Paul's Political Advice," 260; Reese, "Pauline Politics: Rom. 13:1–7," 333. This is probably the more accurate description of the position of these men.

The thesis of this chapter is that every treatment of Romans 13:1–7 that fails to recognize the centrality of the question of revolution has missed the main point of the passage. Such treatments, therefore, are defective at a pivotal point. Paul's precise point in Romans 13:1–7 is to prohibit all revolution and—contrary to Cranfield—to settle the matter! This point has been missed by many modern commentators, not because of any abstruseness in Paul's language but rather due to the inability of the commentators, as Boulton noted, to critique their own political prejudices in light of the passage. The glare of Lockean political ideas has blinded them to the clear teaching of Scripture. An interesting confirmation of this occurs when T. J. Reese, eager to make the point that the demands of the passage are conditional, cites none other than John Locke on Romans. He then provides us with an amazing manifestation of his lack of awareness of his own political roots when he says, "This is remarkably in tune with what contemporary scripture scholars tell us about Paul's ethical teaching in general."[12] Since John Locke is more than a little responsible for what most "contemporary scripture scholars" think about politics, we ought not to be quite as surprised as Mr. Reese that John Locke agrees with them!

II. THE CONTEXT AND OCCASION OF ROMANS 13:1–7

It is customary nowadays to refer to James Kallas's article, "Romans 13:1–7: An Interpolation," during any discussion of the context or occasion of our passage.[13] Kallas's thesis is that Roman 13:1–7 is independent of its context, interrupts it, and even contradicts basic Pauline ideas. It, therefore, is to be regarded as an interpolation.

Kallas's thesis has not found widespread acceptance even among other historical-critical scholars. It is remarkable mainly for the way in which it illustrates how historico-critical assumptions

---

12   Reese, "Pauline Politics: Rom. 13:1–7," 331.
13   J. Kallas, "Romans 13:1–7: An Interpolation," *New Testament Studies*, XI (July 1965).

can blind otherwise reasonable men to the plain exegetical facts of Scripture. One may refer to Cranfield's summary of the many connections between Romans 13:1–7 and its context.[14] For our purposes, the following connections must be noticed.

In the first place, a close connection exists between the vocabulary of 13:1–7 and the vocabulary of the rest of chapters 12 and 13. Of the thirty major vocabulary items that occur in Romans 13:1–7, there are seventeen recurrences in the rest of chapters 12 and 13. None of these uses occur in 12:17–21. Additionally, there is a common rootage of both chapter 12 and 13:1–7 in Old Testament Wisdom.[15] Proverbs is alluded to three times in 12:16–21, while the similarities between 13:1–7 and particularly verses 3 and 4 will become increasingly evident in this book. Perhaps, however, the most striking proof of the intimate relation of 13:1–7 to its context is the repetition of the verb *apodidomai* in 13:7 and 8.

In noticing the many contextual connections of Romans 13:1–7, we have not yet dealt with the question as to whether Paul had any specific occasion for emphasizing the duty of subordination to civil government in his letter to the Romans. James Denney answers this question in the affirmative with these perceptive words, "There is nothing exactly like verses 1—7 elsewhere in Paul's epistles, and it is difficult not to believe that he had some particular reason for treating the question here."[16]

Many theories have been put forward as to the identity of this particular reason.[17] The position advocated here may lay claim to both a long lineage historically and the most adherents numerically.[18] It sees as the occasion of this passage the influence Paul feared

14   C. E. B. Cranfield, "A Commentary on Romans 12–13," *The Scottish Journal of Theology*: Occasional Paper #12 (Edinburgh: Oliver and Boyd, 1965), 61–62.

15   Cranfield, 61–62. See also Murray, *The Epistle to the Romans*, 142.

16   James Denney, *The Expositor's Greek Testament: St. Paul's Epistle to the Romans*, ed. by W. Robertson Nicoll (Grand Rapids: Eerdmans, 1970), 695.

17   Ridderbos, *Paul*, 320, 323; Webster, "St. Paul's Political Advice," 277–282; Paul S. Minear, *The Obedience of Faith* (London: SCM, 1971), 88–90.

18   David Brown, *A Commentary on the Old and New Testaments: Acts-Romans* (Grand Rapids: Eerdmans, 1976), 268; John Calvin, *The Epistle of Paul to the*

Jewish nationalism, with its revolutionary tendencies, might have had on the Christian community at Rome, with its many background connections with the Jewish community in Rome.

Perhaps the most forcible, recent statement of this position is that of Marcus Borg in his article "A New Context for Roman XIII."[19] Notwithstanding the considerable value of this article, it exhibits a danger to be avoided in any discussion of the particular occasion of Romans 13:1–7. This is the danger of an undue specificity which restricts the application of the passage. Borg says in the opening paragraph of his article,

> Even among scholars whose approach to Romans XIII has been to locate it meticulously within its historical context, the chapter has generally been regarded as a source of universally valid principles relating to the Christian concept of civil authority. This article offers an alternative exegesis: an interpretation which depends upon setting Paul's words within the context of Jewish nationalism. Its contention is that Paul's famous generalizations about governing authorities were intended, not as abiding principles to be applied in every situation, but as specific advice to particular people facing an historically identifiable set of circumstances.[20]

This danger is also exhibited in other exegetes.[21]

Such attempts to localize the concern and thereby limit the application of Romans 13 must be rejected for the following reasons:

Romans, trans. by R. Mackinzie (Grand Rapids: Eerdmans, 1979), 8:280; Charles Hodge, *Romans* (London, Banner of Truth, 1972), 405ff.; Denney, *The Expositor's Greek Testament: St. Paul's Epistle to the Romans*, 695; Murray, *The Epistle to the Romans*, 145; Garrett, "The Dialectic of Rom. 13:1–7 and Revelation 13: Part One," 436.

19   Borg, "A New Context for Romans XIII," 205.
20   Borg, 205.
21   Hultgren, "Reflections on Rom. 13:1–7," 263, 269.

1. As will be made clear in this book, the anti-revolutionary thrust of Romans 13 is not the exclusive property of this passage. It is rather the pervasive teaching of both the Old and New Testaments. It cannot thereby be set aside in its normativity as merely an "immediate policy" for negotiating a "specific political crisis."[22]

2. It must also be noted that while Paul had in mind a specific danger, the passage is yet stated in terms that are perfectly general and universal. Perhaps the best illustration of this is the difference of opinion documented above as to the existence and precise character of the danger Paul was addressing.

While there is nothing in the passage to suggest a purely local application for Paul's instructions, there is everything to suggest the opposite. Morrison comments,

> The direct simplicity of the paragraph forbids extreme interpretations. . . . There is no clear limitation of Paul's words to the particular authorities who had jurisdiction over the particular Roman congregation at that particular time. . . . There is no reason to believe that Paul's view of the State would be lightly altered by circumstances; he had suffered and Jesus had been put to death at the hand of the State, but Paul was peculiarly impressed by the hand of God in it all. The absence of any qualification of his words and his unfamiliarity with the local magistrates in Rome suggest that his words in our passage are of a general character.[23]

While the whole of Romans 13:1–7 seems to consist of general affirmations, it is the assertion of verse 1, "for there is no authority except from God," that most clearly and undeniably demonstrates the universal application of the passage. The deduction Paul draws from the assertion just cited confirms its universality. He infers from it that "those which exist are established by God." The

---

22 Borg, "A New Context for Romans XIII," 218.
23 Clinton D. Morrison, *The Powers That Be* (London: SCM, 1960), 105.

thought is clearly that because all authority is from God (that is to say, everywhere and in all circumstances), therefore the particular authorities with which you Romans are dealing are also given their authority by God and so are to be respected.

3. This rebuttal of Borg and others for their undue specificity may be concluded by a brief reflection on the background of their undue localizing of the application of the passage. The conviction must be stated that Borg and others are guilty of a typical, neo-orthodox rupturing of the continuity of history and the unity of the human race (and thus of the continuity and unity characteristic of biblical ethics) in the interest of their (unconscious?) predisposition toward Lockean political concepts.

Before commencing our discussion of the evidence for the Jewish revolutionary danger at Rome, the foregoing caution requires a clarification of the thesis of this chapter. It is, according to our thesis, revolution and rebellion that Paul intends to prohibit in the passage. This is, however, not to say that Paul's exclusive concern was with problems of such magnitude or extremity. Rather, in dealing with these ultimate issues, he makes clear what Christians' attitudes should be on a whole range of lesser issues.

In presenting the evidence for the position that it was Jewish nationalism with its revolutionary tendencies and its influence on Roman Christians that occasioned Romans 13:1–7, the general evidence for Jewish revolutionary tendencies in the first century AD will be reviewed and then its peculiar relevance for Romans 13:1–7 will be examined.

A. The Evidence for Jewish Revolutionary Tendencies in the First Century AD

The New Testament bears abundant witness to the rebelliousness of the Jews toward Roman rule. John Murray writes,

> We know from the N. T. itself that the Jews had
> questions regarding the rights of the Roman

government (cf. Matt. 22:16, 17; Mk. 12:14; Lk. 20:21, 22) We also know that the Jews were disposed to pride themselves on their independence (cf. Jn. 8:33). We read also of seditious movements (Acts 5:36, 37). . . . We are told that Claudius "had commanded all the Jews to depart from Rome" (Acts 18:2). This expulsion must have been occasioned by the belief that Jews were inimical to the imperial interests, if not the aftermath of Jewish insurrection.[24]

To the New Testament evidence mentioned by Murray, the following may be added. Luke 23:19 speaks of Barabbas as "one who had been thrown into prison for a certain insurrection made in the city, and for murder." Luke 13:1 mentions certain Galileans whom Pilate had slaughtered. Since Galilee was a hotbed of Jewish zealotry,[25] and the passage speaks of their blood being mingled with their sacrifices, it is not undue speculation when Cullmann says, "Probably we have to do here with a Zealot uprising."[26] One must also mention the destruction of Jerusalem in AD 70 prophesied by Jesus (see especially Matt 24:15–28 and its parallels). The mentions of false Christs and false prophets in these passages confirm the responsibility of Jewish zealotry for the Jewish rebellion that led to the destruction of Jerusalem. Also interesting is the fact that Peter, the apostle to the circumcision (Gal 2:9), finds it necessary to repeatedly caution his mainly Jewish readers (1 Pet 1:1) against insubordination (1 Pet 2:13–17) or incurring suffering by evildoing, evildoing of an even violent character (3:13–17; 4:14–16). Peter begins this emphasis by remarking, "And who is there to harm you if you prove *zealous* for what is good." (3:13) This is in all probability a veiled reference to the revolutionary zealotry that infected the Jews. One may also mention the significant correlation in Titus, where in 3:1 we have Paul's only other explicit call

---

24   Murray, *The Epistle to the Romans*, 146.
25   S. G. F. Brandon, *Jesus and the Zealots* (New York: Charles Schribner's Sons, 1976), 54, 65, 78, 226, 339.
26   Oscar Cullmann, *The State in the New Testament* (London: SCM, 1957), 14.

for subordination to civil authority. This call is issued after Paul has already expressed a deep concern about "many rebellious men [*anupotaktoi*] . . . especially those of the circumcision . . . [who are] upsetting whole families . . . [by encouraging the Cretans to] . . . pay attention to Jewish myths" (1:10–14). Much more could be said along such lines. Jesus resisted the popular desire to "make him a king by force" (John 6:15) yet was ultimately accused of and crucified under the charge of being the King of the Jews in a political and temporal sense (John 19:19). Both events undoubtedly reflect the political tensions ever present in Judea due to Jewish nationalism. We may conclude this summary of the New Testament evidence by remembering that the ostensible Old Testament justification for such zealotry was readily available in Deuteronomy 17:15, "You shall surely set a king over you whom the LORD your God chooses, one from among your countrymen you shall set as king over yourselves; you may not put a foreigner over yourselves who is not your countryman."

Recent studies have underscored the shadow that the "Jewish national resistance movement" cast over all that was connected with the Jews in the first century, including Jesus and the New Testament.[27] Though marred to a greater or lesser degree by critical perspectives, these studies serve to fill in the background for the New Testament evidence.[28] Borg helpfully summarizes the state of the evidence:

> A considerable amount of recent research has shown that the milieu in which Jesus conducted his ministry was characterized by latent and open conflict between Palestine and Rome and frequent eruptions of particular acts of revolutionary violence against Rome by the national liberation movement. . . . A

27   Borg, "A New Context for Romans XIII"; Brandon, *Jesus and the Zealots*; Cullmann, *The State in the New Testament*; W. R. Farmer, *Maccabees, Zealots, and Josephus* (New York, Columbia University Press, 1956).

28   Brandon, *Jesus and the Zealots;* Cullman, *The State in the New Testament,* respectively.

careful reading of Josephus has always shown this, and the recent discoveries at Qumran add even more evidence for the conflict between Rome and Judaism. In particular, the War Scroll manifests a community which envisaged a future conflict between themselves and Rome; so intense was the hostility that Rome and the Roman forces are explicitly identified as Satan and his hosts.[29]

Particularly interesting in relation to Romans 13:1–7 is the evidence that connects certain sayings of Jesus in Matthew 5:38–48 (Luke 6:27–35) with the violence of Jewish zealotry. Borg asserts, "It is virtually certain that the sayings of Jesus about non-violence and non-retaliation must be interpreted against this background."[30] It is especially the statement of Jesus in Matthew 5:43–44 that has come in for discussion here: "You have heard that it was said, 'You shall love your neighbor and hate your enemy.' But I say to you, love your enemies, and pray for those who persecute you." The critical question here concerns who it was that said, "You shall love your neighbor and hate your enemy." The formula of citation shows it is not the Old Testament that is being cited here.[31] The quotation is not Scripture but Jewish perversion of Scripture.[32] Both Borg and O. J. F. Seitz agree with this and locate the source of such Jewish perversion in the camp of the Jewish revolutionaries. Seitz tells us,

> Careful students of the historical works of Flavius Josephus had long been aware that in his account of the Essenes, as presented in the Jewish War, he stated that anyone seeking admission to that sect was required to promise under oath "always to hate the unrighteous and to contend together at the side of

---

29   Borg, "A New Context for Romans XIII," 205ff.

30   Borg, 205.

31   John Murray, *Principles of Conduct* (Grand Rapids: Eerdmans, 1957), 157ff.

32   Though this is the case, the text, 2 Chr 19:2, is often overlooked and evinces that there were not lacking in the OT elements that could be perverted in the way that Matt 5:43–44 illustrate.

the righteous." Yet one seldom if ever finds this noted in commentaries on Matt. v. 43. Perhaps, like so much else in the assertions of Josephus, this has been taken *cum grano salis*, as an unlikely exaggeration on his part. On the basis of certain reports about the Essenes given by Philo of Alexandria, a facile deduction has occasionally been drawn that these men might be classified as "pacifists." Josephus himself, in the paragraph preceding the above statement, described them as "agents of peace." In spite of such reservations, it now appears entirely probable that the Essene oath of hatred described by Josephus deserves to be taken seriously. Whether or not the writers of the Dead Sea Scrolls were members of that sect, or closely related to it as is commonly supposed, it is noteworthy that exactly such a pledge or obligation is to be found in the so-called Manual of Discipline, or Rule of the Community:

To love all the sons of light, each according to his lot among the council of God, but to hate all the sons of darkness, each according to his guilt in the vengeance of God.

The "sons of darkness" are clearly regarded by the writer not merely as enemies of the Jewish nation, or the sect in particular; they are seen as enemies of God himself, guilty of provoking his ultimate condemnation and retribution. Just who these "sons of darkness" were can be determined more precisely from another scroll which describes in detail preparations for the final war against them by the "sons of light." Prominent among the hostile forces are the armies of the Kittim, a biblical term which there is good reason to believe the scroll-writer adopted to designate the Roman legions. . . . If the writer of this scroll concerning the war of the sons of light was an Essene of some kind, his belligerence toward the Kittim can be matched with a report by

> Josephus regarding a certain John the Essene. This
> man was appointed general . . . during the opening
> years of the War against Rome.[33]

Indications are not lacking in the immediate context of Matthew 5:43 that confirm that the enemies mentioned in Matthew 5:43 were specifically the Roman enemies. There is in the succeeding context the mention of "the tax-gatherers" and the "Gentiles." The term *Gentiles* in Matthew frequently has political connotations and refers to Roman authorities (Matt 10:18; 20:19, 25). The tax-gatherers were, of course, their most hated Jewish collaborators. Further evidence that the Roman enemies are being spoken of in Matthew 5:43 may be found in the preceding context where there is at least one illustration of loving your enemies that explicitly refers to the duty of loving the *Roman* enemies. Verse 41 states, "And whoever shall force you to go one mile, go with him two." An interpreter notes, "The words in Matt. 5:41 . . . refer to the authority of Roman legionaries to commandeer and impress a man into service, such as carrying baggage or other burdens; so Mark 15:21; Matt. 27:32."[34]

In the opinion of this writer, the possibility exists that more of verses 38–42 may find their background in the difficulties faced by the Jews at the hands of the Roman occupational forces. The words of verse 38b ("an eye for an eye and a tooth for a tooth") are in their original Old Testament context a principle of civil law. One can easily see how the assumptions of Jewish nationalism might lead to a usurpation of the rights of civil government. How natural it would be for such a movement to create a shadow government and, consequently, apply this principle in violent action against the Roman authorities.

The interpretation advocated here has the further advantage of delivering the statements of Jesus from application without regard to

---

33   O. J. F. Seitz, "Love Your Enemies," *New Testament Studies* XVI (1969–1970), 49–50.

34   Seitz, 52.

their original context in every conceivable situation. As Borg tells us, on our understanding, "it follows that these sayings are not primarily generalizations about passive non-resistance but are spoken to a concrete situation counselling his hearers not to join in armed resistance to Rome."[35]

The bottom line of all this is that the main intent, or at least one intent, of Jesus in the sayings of Matthew 5:38–48 was to quell any revolutionary tendencies among His followers. But what has all this to do with Romans 13:1–7? Much in every way! "There is a strong affinity of subject matter between the synoptic words of Jesus that have just been cited and Rom. 12:14–21," Borg informs us.[36] Specifically, Romans 12:14 echoes Matthew 5:44 and 5:39. As the earlier treatment of the context of Romans 13:1–7 has made clear, there is a complex network of connections that literally tie Romans 13:1–7 to 12:14–21. One must also note the direct link between Romans 13:2 and Matthew 5:39 in the double repetition of *anthisteimi* in Romans 13:2, the keyword of Matthew 5:39. Borg raises the question that this close connection between Romans 13:1–7 and Matthew 5:38–48 suggests:

> In the Palestinian milieu in which Jesus taught and in which the Semitic code took shape, we have already argued that "Love your enemies" referred to disavowal of a militant anti-Roman policy. Is it possible that it also has this intention here, that Paul is telling the Roman church to avoid entanglement in an anti-Roman policy? If so, then Romans xiii. 1-7, which follow immediately upon this code, would naturally be interpreted in the same context: do not attach yourselves to the militant policy advocated by certain Jewish groups.[37]

---

35   Borg, "A New Context for Romans XIII," 207.
36   Borg, 207.
37   Borg, 207.

B. *The Peculiar Relevance of This for Romans 13:1–7*

In a copiously footnoted section of his article, Borg details the evidence for the peculiar relevance of Jewish revolutionary tendencies for the church at Rome. Lengthy portions of that section must now be quoted:

> In order to affirm that these words are intended by Paul to carry the same meaning as they did in the ministry of Jesus, we would have to show that the Roman congregation needed this advice; that is, that it or a considerable portion of it might have been tempted to adopt an antagonistic attitude toward the Roman state.
>
> It is common to say that we know very little about the church at Rome at the time when Paul wrote. What we do know is that it had a fair number of Jews in it. The fourth-century writer Ambrosiaster cites a tradition that the Christian community in Rome rose among Roman Jews who then evangelized Gentiles, a tradition indirectly supported by Acts ii. 10, which reports the presence of Roman Jews among the pilgrims at Pentecost. The contents of the epistle point to a mixed Gentile and Jewish membership, with perhaps a slightly greater degree of Jewish influence than in the churches founded by Paul. Further, it is probable on *a priori* grounds that many of the Gentile members were originally attached to the synagogues as "God-fearers", so that even they had an original association with Judaism. Judaism and Jewish communities constituted the matrix of Christianity. The Christian tradition and the sociocultural characteristics of Christian communities eventually evolved away from their Jewish origins, but it would be naive to suppose that after only two decades of Christian history any community incorporating Jews in its foundation

was largely detached from Jewish affairs. Roman authorities were sociologically justified in the fifties in their policy of regarding Christianity as a Jewish sect. Hence events which affected the Roman Jewish community could be expected to be of concern to the Christian community in Rome as well. Thus there are solid grounds for assuming that we can learn something about the Roman church by asking about the Roman Jewish community.

We must ask two questions about the Jewish community in Rome. Was there continuing contact between Jews in Rome and Palestine so that the chaotic events in the homeland were known about among Roman Jews? Second, was the Roman community subject to some of the same stresses as were Jews in Palestine so that there existed from time to time a common bond of anti-Roman sentiment?

To the first question, several factors point conclusively to an affirmative answer. For all Jews, Jerusalem was the geographic centre of their faith. The 50,000 Roman Jews, like other Jews, paid the temple tax and went on pilgrimage to Jerusalem, where there was even a synagogue assigned to Roman "libertini". Large numbers of Roman Jews were either former Jewish prisoners of war or descendants of prisoners taken captive by Rome in various campaigns. Delegations from Palestine to Rome were frequent and both Herod Agrippa and his son were residents in Rome. Moreover, Rome as the imperial capital was the centre for political, cultural, and economic traffic. All ideas, like all roads, ran to Rome, and especially when an audience of 50,000 awaited them. We may thus conclude that events in Palestine were known about by Roman Jews.

To the second question an equally positive answer can be given. In 4 B.C., in the succession controversy following the death of Herod the Great, two events point to the sympathy of Roman Jews for Jewish nationalist sentiments. While the sons of Herod presented their case in Rome to Augustus, a delegation of fifty Palestinian Jews arrived to plead with Augustus that Palestine should be placed under a governor sent from Rome rather than remaining under the control of the Herods. 8,000 Roman Jews supported the delegation and opposed Archelaus. Initially, the Jewish request for a Roman governor appears to be anti-nationalist in spirit, but this superficial impression is corrected by the perception that the Herods were detested as non-Jewish kings who had no right to the throne. Moreover, the Sanhedrin could be expected to enjoy considerable autonomy under a Roman governor, far more than under Herod, who had executed members of the Sanhedrin. Indeed, Josephus himself used the word "autonomy" to describe the goal which their request sought, a return of control of Jewish domestic life from the non-Jewish Herods to the Jewish senate. That the Jews of Rome supported this request in opposition to the heirs of Herod, who had adorned (or desecrated) Palestine with lavish monuments to Rome and who was known as the friend of Rome, is highly significant. The second event in the same year is the nearly delirious reception which Roman Jews gave to the impostor who arrived in Rome to claim the Judean throne, pretending to be Alexander, Herod's son by Mariamme. Why such enthusiasm for a presumed son of Herod when the other sons of Herod had so recently been opposed by the Jewish enclave in Rome? Because Alexander (the real one, that is) had Hasmonean blood in his veins through his mother Mariamme, i.e., he was among the last of the Maccabees, whose memory was one pillar of Jewish nationalism.

But the anti-Roman sentiments of Roman Jews did not need to feed solely upon sympathy with the aspirations of Palestinian Jews. For, despite the vaunted role of the empire as the *de jure* protector of Jewish rights, Roman Jews frequently suffered directly from both official Roman policy and the generalized anti-Semitism of the Mediterranean world. Under the three emperors prior to the time when Paul wrote to Rome, Roman Jews suffered expulsion under Tiberius in A.D. 19, twelve years of anti-Semitic policy in Italy under Tiberius' closest adviser Sejanus, the threat of annihilation through the insane hatred of Caligula, and the inconsistent policies of Claudius, who finally expelled them again in A.D. 49. Their exile apparently lasted five years until the beginning of the reign of Nero, only one to five years before Paul wrote to Rome.

That the Roman Jews, even apart from sympathy for the plight of their compatriots in Palestine, had cause to distrust Rome is obvious. Yet events in Palestine during the forties and fifties could only reinforce antipathy toward Rome. Under the procurator Fadus (A.D. 44–6), several Jewish revolutionary leaders were executed, including the two sons of Judas who founded the "fourth philosophy" in A.D. 6. Possibly in the same year as Claudius' edict expelling the Jews from Rome, some of the most serious disturbances prior to the war of A.D. 6670 broke out in Palestine; according to Josephus, thousands of Jews were killed at Passover following an insulting gesture by a Roman soldier on the roof of the temple; moreover, a Roman soldier destroyed a copy of the Torah, an action reminiscent of the days of Antiochus Epiphanes. Throughout the fifties, Cumanus (A.D. 48–52) and Felix (A.D. 52–60) faced Jewish revolutionaries, crucifying some and engaging in armed battle with others.

What was the reaction of the Roman Jewish community to these events in Palestine prior to the time when Paul wrote? Suetonius' statement regarding Claudius' edict is the only evidence for activity within the Jewish community at the time: *Iudaeos impulsore Chresto assidue tumultuantes Toma expulit*—"Since the Jews constantly made disturbances at the instigation of Chrestus, he [Claudius] expelled them from Rome.". . .

That this was a concern of the Roman church is confirmed by the content of Romans as a whole. It must be noted first that the question of Israel receives more emphasis in Romans than in any other Pauline letter, a curiosity which is explained by the above account of the Roman church. More pointedly, Paul eventually answers directly the particular question which we have adduced, but he precedes it with a theological substructure on the status of Israel in which he handles two prior and relevant questions. Does Israel have some special claim on God's grace which commits God to preserving their particularity and separateness, that is, their nationhood? If so, then engagement in precipitate action against Rome to preserve that nationhood makes sense, for God's help can be expected. Alternatively, if she has no special claim on God, are her sufferings then a sign that she has been rejected by God?

To the first question, Paul answers with an emphatic negative. Those features to which first-century Judaism commonly pointed as signs of God's special favour are systematically reviewed and reinterpreted in such a way as to nullify their national significance: the confidence that God's judgment means punishment primarily for the Gentiles (ii. 110); possession of the Torah (ii. 1124); circumcision (ii. 259); descent from Abraham (iv. 115, ix. 6ff). None of these commits God to preserving Israel's

particularity, her nationhood; for all, Jew and Gentile
alike, have sinned, and all, Jew and Gentile, are now
justified in the same way by God's gracious act in
Jesus Christ (i. 16,11. 910, iii.9, 234, 2930). So the
foundation stone for precipitate action is destroyed.
But if Israel has no special claim on God's grace,
do her present sufferings mean that she has been
rejected so that there is no Christian obligation to
Israel? The answer is equally emphatic: by no means;
and the extensive section in chapters ixxi deals with
this question.[38]

To the scholarship of Borg, the following remarks may be added
to confirm the peculiar relevance of the danger under discussion
to the Roman church. It is indisputable that Jewish Christians of
a very conservative nature are among the recipients of the letter to
the Romans. Inculcating the unity of the Spirit between Jew and
Gentile is one of the main goals of the letter. Recent discussion
has focused on Paul's repeated affirmation of the principle "There
is no distinction" (see Rom 1:17; 3:22, 29–30; 4:16; 5:12–21;
10:12–13). This principle is at the heart of Paul's discussion of sin
and redemption in chapters 1–8. It gives rise to the problem Paul
tackles in chapters 9–11. If there is no distinction, what do we
make of God's promises to the Jews? This principle is also basic to
the more pervasively hortatory section, 12:1–15:13. It grounds the
love and mutual service demanded in 12:1–13:14. More signifi-
cantly, it is the foundation for the exhortation to unity addressed
to the strong (Gentiles) and the weak (Jews) in 14:1–15:13. This
section begins only eight verses after the conclusion of the passage
under discussion and may form the practical conclusion and focus
of the letter. It must be noted with reference to this section that
it is not improbable that those with distinctive Jewish tendencies
regarding food, drink, and days would also exhibit distinctively
Jewish tendencies regarding politics![39]

---

38   Borg, 208–214.
39   Minear, *The Obedience of Faith*, 88–90.

The conclusion must be that the foregoing evidence puts beyond a reasonable doubt that Paul wrote Romans 13:1–7 with the intention of forestalling Jewish revolutionary influence in the Roman congregation. Paul meets this threat not with specific arguments but with a general prohibition of revolutionary activity. To the details of Paul's anti-revolutionary response to Jewish nationalism, this book now turns.

III. THE MEANING OF SUBORDINATION

In this section and the following this chapter takes up the actual content of Romans 13:1–7. It is not the intention of these sections to exegete systematically every grammatical problem in this passage. Rather, its purpose is to set in relief those aspects of the content of Romans 13:1–7 that make clear its anti-revolutionary intention. Having seen the anti-revolutionary context of Romans 13:1–7, we move now to its anti-revolutionary content.

The thesis regarding the meaning of subordination we will argue is that the call to subordination (*hupotassestho*, v. 1; *hupotassesthai* v. 5) is intended primarily as a prohibition of rebellion. Subordination, it is maintained, designates the civil virtue that has for its contrasting vice, armed rebellion. This thesis will be developed via the examination of the word itself, the meaning of the contrasting terminology, the confirmatory significance of verses 6 and 7, and concluding with an examination of the question of exceptions to the Pauline prohibition.

A. The Meaning of the Word Itself

It is customary for exegetes to interpret the verb *hupatasso*, used in verses 1 and 5, as the simple equivalent of *obedience*. Probably the majority of commentators do this. *The Living Bible* translates the verb this way. One exegete confesses, in fact, after considering Cranfield's treatment of the verb, that he can see no difference between *obedience* and *subordination*.[40]

---

40 Reese, "Pauline Politics: Rom. 13:1–7," 330.

It cannot, of course, be denied that subordination and obedience are closely related and that ordinarily the former entails the latter. Simply equating subordination with obedience, however, represents a significant trivializing of Paul's concern and neutering of his language in Romans 13. Speaking of Romans 13 as simply requiring obedience reflects a superficial idea of what Paul is requiring. Thankfully, there are a number of interpreters who have recently underscored the distinction. Cranfield, Yoder, Bruce, and John Murray are among such men.[41]

Obedience is seldom an adequate translation for *hupotasso* in the New Testament. In certain cases, it is, in fact, difficult to see how such a translation would make any sense at all (see 1 Pet 3:22; Rom 8:20; 1 Cor 14:32, 34; Luke 10:17, 20.) One certainly cannot think of willing obedience in the case of Luke 10:17, 20 or 1 Peter 3:22.

As both the etymology and usage of the word make clear, *hupotasso* denotes the being of one under an order, i.e., an authority. In the middle (the probable sense in Rom 13:1), it means to put oneself under an authoritative order. In the passive it means to be put under an authority. Clearly, only in the middle does *hupotasso* approach the idea of obedience and that only very approximately. The idea of an authoritative order contained in *hupotasso* is emphasized in Romans 13:1–2 by the use of three other words derived from the *tasso* root, which itself means to fix, determine, or order. *Antitassomenos* means to set oneself against an order, to resist an authority. *Diatage* means "ordinance" and is a reference here to civil authority as ordered by God. *Tetagemai* itself in this context speaks of God's ordination or ordering of the civil authorities. The idea of an authoritative order is also prominent in the other occurrences of *hupotasso* in the New Testament. It is used with

---

41   Cranfield, "A Commentary on Romans 12–13," 69f.; Yoder, *The Politics of Jesus*, 212; Murray, *The Epistle to the Romans*, 148; F. F. Bruce, "Paul and 'The Powers That Be,'" *Bulletin of the John Ryland Library*, LXVI (Spring, 1984), 78–96; R. A. Sabath, "Paul's View of the State," The Post-American, (April, 1974), III, 8–11.

reference to the authority of parents (x1), husbands (x5), males (x1), civil government (x2), slave masters (x2), the Messiah (x12), God (x1), the law of God (x1), and the righteousness of God (x1). Murray is right: "The term for subjection is more inclusive than that for obedience. It implies [I would add the word *normally*] obedience when ordinances to be obeyed are in view, but there is more involved. Subjection indicates the recognition of our subordination in the whole realm of the magistrates' jurisdiction and willing subservience to their authority."[42]

It is difficult to conceive a word that would more precisely check revolutionary attitudes and encourage their precise opposite than *hupotasso*. Far from promoting violently attacking the civil authorities, rejecting and removing them, this word encourages calm acquiescence in and acceptance of our subordinate status.

This leads us to an observation that forms a transition to our next point. The antonyms of *hupotasso* in the New Testament are not words signifying mere disobedience. Rather, it is contrasted with actual enmity or hostility (*exthros*) in Romans 8:7, and in James 4:7, the contrast is with opposing, withstanding, or resisting (*anthisteimi*), a word with warlike connotations. This same word is contrasted with *hupotasso* in Romans 13:2.

B. The Meaning of the Contrasting Terminology

Perhaps the clearest way to illustrate the difference between *subordination* and *obedience* is simply to ask, What are their opposites? Is the opposite of subordination disobedience? Clearly not! It is insubordination or, to use the language of Romans 13:2, resistance (*antitasso*) and opposition (*anthisteimi*). We must now examine the meaning of these words in more detail.

1. Resistance—Antitasso

The etymology and usage of *antitasso* clearly identifies its meaning as setting oneself against an authoritative order. It is distinctly the

---

42   Murray, *The Epistle to the Romans*, 148.

antonym of *hupotasso*. There is, however, little by way of biblical background to expand our understanding of this word. It is used only five times in the New Testament and only six times in the LXX of the Old Testament. To be sure, it is clearly a far more forceful word than disobedience—see Acts 18:6, "They resisted and blasphemed," and James 5:6, "You have put to death the righteous man; he does not resist you." Equally clear is the fact that it cannot possibly be a synonym for disobedience—see James 4:6 and 1 Peter 5:5, "God is opposed to the proud." Moulton and Milligan's discussion of its extra-biblical use during the New Testament era does, however, shed light on its connotations. They comment that it is used two times in accounts of legal proceedings to refer to the opposing party. Even more interestingly, they say, "There are several instances in OGIS in a military sense which was of course the earliest."[43] *Antitasso* very fitly describes the activity of Jewish revolutionaries. This fitness is even more clear with regard to *anthisteimi*.

2. Opposition—Anthisteimi

Again, and even more clearly, this word is no mere synonym for *disobedience* in the New Testament. See Luke 21:15, Acts 6:10, and Galatians 2:11; 6:13. In these texts, the translation of the word with *disobedience* would be simple nonsense. *Anthisteimi* also has clearly marked military overtones in the New Testament (see Gal 6:13; 1 Pet 5:9; Jas 4:7). It is the use of this word in the LXX, however, that makes its characteristic meaning indisputable. Scores of times and in the vast majority of uses it literally describes armed defiance of an attacking enemy (see Lev 26:37; Num 10:9; 22:23, 31, 34; Deut 7:24; 9:2; 11:25; 25:18; 28:7; Josh 1:5; 7:13; 23:9; Judg 2:14; 2 Sam 5:6).

One must conclude that when such a word is used of opposition to civil authorities who themselves are said to bear the sword, it must designate strictly and primarily armed rebellion and violent

---

43   James Hope Moulton and George Milligan, *The Vocabulary of the Greek Testament* (Grand Rapids: Eerdmans, 1982), 49.

revolution. Granted, Paul may intend via this condemnation of the extremes of insubordination to condemn its lesser forms, but the denotative starting point of this word is clearly armed rebellion.

C. *The Confirmatory Significance of Verses 6 and 7*

It is Paul's prohibition of revolution that leads him in verses 6 and 7 to speak of the obligation of paying taxes. The many grammatical and syntactical questions connected with these verses do not concern us here. The single focus of our present interest is that refusal to pay taxes, as even the well-known Boston Tea Party illustrates, has been a characteristic mark of revolution in every age. More cogently, the refusal to pay taxes is connected with Jewish zealotry in the New Testament. It is commonly acknowledged that Paul is building on and alluding to one of those passages in Romans 13:6–7. That passage is Luke 20:25 and its parallels. Note the repetition of *apodidomai* and the conceptual parallels between the two passages. Another passage relevant here is Luke 23:2. Both passages reflect revolutionary tensions in Judea and possess revolutionary overtones. Cullmann explains:

> Luke is probably right in bringing the saying about taxpaying into direct connection with the trial and condemnation of Jesus. In Luke 23:2 we hear that the Jews brought Jesus before Pilate with this accusation: "We found this man inciting our people and forbidding them to pay tribute to Caesar." This means, in other words, he is a leader of the Zealots. The fact that it was possible intentionally to misinterpret Jesus' saying (Mark 12:13) in this way proves that Jesus' answer was complex.
>
> We know that it was just this question of tax-paying which was regarded by Zealots as the criterion, so to speak, of loyalty to Judaism. As a matter of fact, the question was indeed addressed to Jesus in order to "entrap him in his talk" (Mark 12:13). According

to Mark, it is the Pharisees and the Herodians who pose the question. Both groups are at one in wanting Jesus disarmed. And this is the only thing they have in common, for in other matters they are radically opposed. The question is: "Should we pay tribute to Caesar or not?" For themselves, the Pharisees would prefer to answer in the negative, although they do not, like the Zealots, draw the extreme consequences. The Herodians, on the contrary, are the collaborationists who make common cause with the Romans and naturally for themselves return an affirmative answer. It is just the presence of both groups which constitutes for Jesus the special temptation. Both want him to compromise himself. If he answers yes, he will be shown up as a collaborationist and will disillusion the majority of the people; for it is precisely in this connection that these have rested such great hope in him. If he answers no, this is an avowal that he himself is a Zealot, and indeed a leader of the Zealots; and we know what that meant to the Romans.[44]

Cullmann's comments manifest how close to the heart of Jewish nationalism and zealotry the question of the payment of taxes to the Roman authorities was. No wonder, then, that Paul chose to illustrate his demand for subordination and the rejection of rebellion by insisting on the fact that taxes were a debt and obligation owed to the Roman authorities in the concluding verses of the passage. Again, in verses 6 and 7, Paul's central concern is clearly the negation of revolutionary tendencies among the Roman Christians.

D. *The Question of Exceptions*

Having clearly set before us the true significance of the demand for universal subordination to civil authorities, we are now in a position to properly assess the question of whether Paul intended

---

44   Cullmann, *The State in the New Testament*, 34–35.

or would have permitted any exceptions to this demand. Several different questions present themselves:

1. Is conscientious disobedience to civil authority an exception?
It ought to go without saying that Paul "would have endorsed and practised the word of Peter . . . 'we must obey God rather than men' (Acts 5:29, cf. 4:19, 20)."[45]

The real question is this: Is the conscientious disobedience mandated by the Scriptures when the Christian is called upon to sin by a civil authority an exception to the requirement of Romans 13:1–2? More precisely, is such conscientious disobedience insubordination, rebellion, or incipient revolution? The answer clearly must be negative! Conscientious disobedience to certain of the demands of ordained human authorities is clearly consistent with the strictest subordination to their general authority. Lenski sees the matter very clearly when he asserts, "Refusal to obey was not in any way standing against the arrangement of God and the governmental authority this high court possessed."[46] An analogy will helpfully illustrate Lenski's point. A Christian wife is not being rebellious or insubordinate when she refuses to sin at the behest of her husband. To accuse such a wife of rebellion would be the grossest injustice. Here Yoder has perceptively stated the point:

> It is not by accident that the imperative of 13:1 is not literally one of obedience. The Greek language has good words to denote *obedience*, in the sense of completely bending one's will and one's actions to the desires of another. What Paul calls for, however, is subordination. The verb is based on the same root as the ordering of the powers of God. Subordination is significantly different from obedience. The conscientious objector who refuses to do what his

---

45 Murray, *The Epistle to the Romans*, 149.
46 R. C. H. Lenski, *St. Paul's Epistle to the Romans* (Minneapolis: Augsburg, 1961), 788. In the context, Lenski is commenting on Acts 5:29.

> government asks him to do, but still remains under the sovereignty of that government and accepts the penalties which it imposes, or the Christian who refuses to worship Caesar but still permits Caesar to put him to death, is being subordinate even though he is not obeying.[47]

All this is not mere logomachy. Our point is that conscientious disobedience is not an exception to Romans 13:1. It is not resisting or opposing the civil authority. It is not revolution. Conscientious disobedience cannot be used to prove the necessity of making exceptions to Romans 13:1. The exception of just rebellion cannot be sneaked in the door with the exception of conscientious disobedience. This sets the stage for the next question to be raised.

2. Would Paul permit any exceptions to his prohibition of rebellion?

The first and most obvious thing that must be said here is that there is nothing in Romans 13:1–7 to encourage a positive answer to this question and everything to suggest a negative. The imperative itself is emphatically universal, "Let every soul." While Paul may be thinking only of Christian "souls," the imperative is distributively universal within the Christian community, and there is no reason to think unbelievers do not have a similar obligation. The ground of the imperative is also universal, "for there is no authority except from God, and those which exist are established by God." The authorities to which one submits may not be chosen at one's whim. Every authority is from God. Precisely the ones with whom the Romans now have to do, the ones that now exist, they are to subordinate themselves to. This means also that the phrase *echousiais huperexousais* may not be translated "the supreme authorities." It is *authorities* plural that are in view. In the Roman Empire, there could be only one supreme authority (see 1 Pet 2:13). Hence this phrase, as Cranfield remarks, designates

---

47   Yoder, *The Politics of Jesus*, 212.

the authorities as superior not to other authorities but to those whom they govern.[48] We may paraphrase, "the authorities which are over you." The subordinate relation of the Roman Christians to the authorities God has put over them is emphasized. To these remarks may be added the observation that the statements of Paul throughout these verses give every appearance of being completely general in their application.

The actual powers to whom Paul was referring were neither Christian nor unusually moral. To be sure, it is probable that Paul wrote before Nero manifested his true colors, but surely the reigns of Claudius and Caligula had sufficiently manifested the depravity of the Roman beast, particularly to Jewish revolutionaries. Further, the position that Paul's attitude would have changed after Nero's degeneration must, with Ridderbos, be flatly rejected:

> In explanation of this very positive attitude, some have pointed to the favorable experience of Paul with the Roman government. Others have said that he would not have written these words if he had foreseen the coming persecution under Nero, etc. But in the first place such a conception attributes to Paul a naively optimistic evaluation of the existing political order that bears no relationship to what he himself had already experienced and to what since the death of Jesus had repeatedly been the experience of the Christian church. In the second place, it is completely in conflict with the fundamental definition of his position, which is not founded in the first instance on what is to be expected from the civil authorities, but what one owes them for God's sake.[49]

The fact that Paul explicitly requires subordination to imperial Rome must be faced by those who condition subordination to any given civil government on its conformity to certain standards.

---

48   Cranfield, "A Commentary on Romans 12–13," 68.
49   Ridderbos, *Paul*, 322.

This leads to a further observation. The Bible nowhere preceptively requires or permits armed rebellion against the existing civil authorities. The fact is that the whole drift of scriptural exhortation is in the direction of encouraging subordination to the existing authorities.[50]

Also significant is the fact that the Bible never implicitly or explicitly provides us with any standard *as a condition for our continued subordination* to any given government. On the contrary, there is biblical precept and example of subordination to and even participation in governments that grossly deviated from the standards of God's moral law. The evidence for these assertions has been cited in a previous chapter.

Finally and conclusively, it must be underscored that the Bible repeatedly and explicitly forbids revolution. David's restraint with reference to the government of Saul is most instructive with reference to the sinfulness of armed rebellion against the servants of God. Surely if anyone ever had the right of armed rebellion, it was David when he was unjustly and violently pursued by Saul. Surely if any ruler had ever forfeited his authority by his transgressions of the law of God, it was Saul, whom God had rejected! Yet we read in 1 Samuel 24:5 that even when David refrained from assassinating Saul and merely cut off the edge of his robe, his conscience was smitten because of the dishonor he had offered "the Lord's anointed" (see also 1 Sam 26:1–12.) If it is objected that Saul was the "Lord's anointed," the reply is in order that Romans 13:1–7 teaches that every civil ruler is in a certain sense the same.

Also relevant in the present connection are two passages in Old Testament Wisdom. The positive calls of that literature for subordination to civil authority have already been cited above. To them must be added two explicit warnings against joining with revolutionaries, Ecclesiastes 8:2–5 and Proverbs 24:21–22. The latter passage is the most important: "My son, fear the LORD and

---

50   See Prov 14:35; 16:10a; 13–15; 19:12; 20:2, 8; 22:11; 24:21–22; 25:2–3, 6–7, 15; 29:4; Eccl 8:2–5; 10:4; Titus 3; 1 Pet 2:13f.; 1 Tim 2:1f.

the king; do not associate with those who are given to change; for their calamity will rise suddenly, and who knows the ruin that cones from both of them?" The conceptual parallels with Romans 13:1–7 are apparent.

The New Testament is equally clear. Deservedly famous are Jesus's words of warning to Peter at the time of his arrest. "Put your sword back into its place; for all those who take up the sword shall perish by the sword." Interestingly enough, the term for *sword* used in this text is identical to that used in our passage. This could be a prohibition of usurping the sword, which God has given exclusively to civil rulers.

Even more significant is Jesus's explicit renunciation of the sword in John 18:36 (cf. vv. 10 and 11). The question must be asked. If Jesus would not permit the use of the sword to prevent the greatest injustice of all time, His crucifixion, then what occasion may justify armed revolt against the existing authorities?

John 18:10–11 and 36 take on an even increased significance when John 19:10–11 are set next to them and compared with Romans 13:1–7. John 19:10–11 reads, "Pilate therefore said to Him, 'You do not speak to me? Do you not know that I have authority to release You, and I have authority to crucify You? Jesus answered, 'You would have no authority over Me, unless it had been given you from above; for this reason, he who delivered Me up to you has the greater sin.'" The occurrence several times in these verses of the word *exousia* also used repeatedly in Romans 13:1–7, is suggestive of the striking parallels between these words and Romans 13:1–7:

1. In both, the civil rulers are acknowledged to have *exousia*, even to the point of using the sword to put to death offenders.

2. In both, it is stressed that this *exousia* is from God.

3. In both, therefore, armed resistance against the *exousia* is forbidden.

Such parallels can scarcely be coincidental and clearly suggest that in Romans 13:1–7 we are face to face with a uniform demand of Scripture to which no exceptions are allowed.

Undoubtedly, such a conclusion cuts across the grain of our inherited Lockean political assumptions, but we must resist the temptation to stretch the Bible to fit our preconceptions. There are, however, two qualifying remarks that, while not constituting exceptions to Romans 13:1–7, do alleviate certain misunderstandings of the biblical ethic.

3. Subordination implies the idea of a defined jurisdiction or sphere of authority when used of human orders.

The term *hupotasso* contains, as noted before, the idea of an authoritative order. In biblical thought, no such order is absolute and unlimited except that of God. He has ordained a number of human authorities each with its own defined and peculiar area of jurisdiction. The civil authority, like the parental and ecclesiastical, is limited in its jurisdiction. Neither the parental nor the ecclesiastical authorities are per se subjected to it. Erastianism is not the theory of the Bible. This, of course, is the lesson of Luke 20:25, "Render to Caesar the things that are Caesar's, and to God the things that are God's." In other words, there are some things that do not belong to Caesar. As noted previously, the language of Luke 20:25 is echoed in Romans 13:6–7. Consequently, the language of verse 7, "Render to all what is due them," implies the same lesson. Hence, though the civil authority may never be attacked, it may be disobeyed when it seeks from us obedience that would require us to sin or when it seeks to impose its power outside its assigned sphere. Of course, the civil authority in disobedience to the divine norms may bring civil sanctions against those who so disobey. Even then, revolt is not an option. The Christian may flee or suffer, but he may never resist or oppose the existing authorities.

4. Romans 13 does not address every difficulty that may be raised about the Christian's civil allegiance.

Romans 13:1–7 makes no attempt to address some difficulties. Legitimate questions sometimes exist as to whom the legitimate representative of the state really is or even as to which government is really the existing authority. Such issues clearly constitute difficult questions that are not at issue in our passage and do not touch the question of revolution. Revolution is armed resistance against *the existing authorities.* Paul's prohibition of such assumes clearly identifiable existing authorities. In most cases, this assumption is not problematic.[51]

IV. The Meaning of Ordination

The rejection of all armed opposition to the existing civil authorities has frequently (although not exclusively) been associated with the Anabaptist tradition and its view that the distinctive functions of the state (particularly its use of the sword) are per se sinful, not meeting with divine approval. Yoder's treatment of the divine ordination of the civil authorities in Romans 13:1–7 is expressive of this viewpoint:

> God is not said to *create* or *institute* or *ordain* the powers that be, but only to *order* them, to put them in order, sovereignly to tell them where they belong, what is their place. It is not as if there was a time when there was no government and then God made government through a new creative intervention; there has been hierarchy and authority and power since human society existed. Its exercise has involved domination, disrespect for human dignity, and real or potential violence ever since sin has existed. Nor is it that in his ordering of it he specifically, morally approves of what government does. The sergeant does not produce the soldiers he drills, the

---

51 Murray, *The Epistle to the Romans*, 150.

librarian does not create nor approve of the book he catalogs and shelves. Likewise, God does not take the responsibility for the existence of the rebellious "powers that be" or for their shape or identity; they already are. What the text says is that he orders them, brings them into line, that by his permissive government he lines them up with his purpose. This is true of all governments.[52]

Yoder's comments raise the question now to be addressed. In what sense are the existing civil authorities fixed or determined by God? Such a discussion presupposes one's doctrine of the will of God. In conformity with the Reformed tradition, the writer believes that there is taught in the Scriptures a twofold conception of the will of God. There is the *decretive* will of God that determines "whatever comes to pass" and which is the standard according to which all things do occur (see Rom 9:19; Acts 4:27–28; Isa 46:10–11; Gen 50:20). There is the *preceptive* will of God, which is the moral standard for human conduct (see John 7:17; Rom 12:2). The decretive will of God is not the ethical standard of human conduct. In fact, while acting in perfect conformity to God's decretive will, one may be grievously violating God's moral standards (see Gen 50:20; Acts 4:27–28).

The difficulty in Romans 13:1 is that *tasso,* the root of *tetagmenai,* may be used to designate both aspects of the divine will, like other similar terms. If *tasso* is used to describe some act of the decretive will of God in Romans 13:2, then Yoder's basic conception would be correct. There are, in fact, not lacking indications that seem to point in such a direction. The fact that all the existing civil authorities are said to be ordained of God appears to point this way since it suggests God's general providence, an aspect of the decretive will of God.

There are conclusive reasons, however, to concur with John Murray when he asserts, "The propositions that the authorities are

---

52   Yoder, *The Politics of Jesus,* 203–204.

of God and ordained of God are not to be understood as referring merely to God's decretive will."[53]

First of all, such a view fails to see that one is morally bound before God to conform one's moral conduct to this expression of the will of God. God's decretive will, by itself, does not constitute a rule for human conduct. One must, therefore, conclude that in *tetagmenai* is an expression of God's preceptive will. This reality is indicated by the close relationship between *tasso* used to describe God's will and used to describe our duty.

Secondly, not only does God's ordering the existing civil authorities ground our duty but also the duty of the civil authorities toward God. It may be granted that Paul never stresses this explicitly in this passage. It is, however, implied in the designations of the civil authorities as the "ministers" and "servants of God." While it is barely conceivable that Paul meant this in a "decretive" sense, (that is, that God in overruling their actions providentially makes them even against their will His ministers and servants) it is far more natural and accordant with the description of them in this passage (as punishing the evil and rewarding the good) to conclude that as God's servants, they are subject to God's preceptive will. More conclusively, it must surely be remembered that Paul's conception of civil authority is erected on the foundation of Old Testament teaching. The pervasive teaching of Old Testament Wisdom is that civil rulers are bound to conform to the norms of God's law and are subject to God's punishment for not conforming.[54]

Yoder's presentation of the Anabaptist doctrine of the state must, therefore, be rejected. Nonetheless, questions hover around Paul's assertion that the existing Roman authorities are ordained of God. Paul, it must be noted, has combined in an unusual way

---

53   Murray, *The Epistle to the Romans*, 148; see also the comments Murray made in his review of an Anabaptist author, *Collected Writings of John Murray*, ed. by Iain Murray (Edinburgh: Banner of Truth, 1982), 3:322f.

54   See Ps 58:1–11; 82:1–8; Prov 16:10, 12; 17:7, 26; 18:5; 20:26, 28; 25:2–3, 5; 28:15–16; 29:4, 12, 14; 31:1–9.

the concepts of general providence and preceptive will in his assertions of verse 2. Can anything more be discerned of the origin
of this unusual conception? We believe something more can be
discerned, something that ties this subject directly to the problem
of revolutionary Jewish nationalism!

One must begin by noting that Jewish revolutionary nationalism was religiously motivated and grounded on theocratic premises. It is particularly Deuteronomy 17:15, as noted, that grounds
their position. In recent studies the Jewish national resistance
movement has received quite a positive evaluation from scholars.[55]
What has not been appreciated in this reaction against Josephus
and his denigration of the Zealots is that Jesus and the New Testament are as anti-Zealot as Josephus. Jesus predicted the judgment
of God on and the disastrous failure of Jewish resistance (see Matt
23:37f.) Stephen apparently echoed his sentiments (Acts 6:14;
Acts 7). In the New Testament, then, there is not simply a sympathetic distancing of its position from the Zealot cause but actually
a withering denunciation of it.

Given the Old Testament authority that could be cited for the
Zealot cause, and given the evident authority the Old Testament
had for Jesus and His apostles, how is this rejection of Zealotry to
be explained?

Our conviction is that Jesus and His apostles understood the
Zealot ideal as but another illustration of the arrogant and stiff-
necked resisting of the Holy Spirit that had characterized the
Jews from the beginning (see Acts 7:51).[56] It was arrogant and
stiff-necked resistance to the divine will because it was a stub-
born refusal to accept the fact that in fulfillment of the curses
of the old covenant, God himself had destroyed the theocratic
kingdom and transferred the civil authority over His people to
the Gentile kingdoms. This, on the clear evidence of the Old
Testament prophets, had occurred when Jerusalem was captured

---

55   Farmer, *Maccabees, Zealots, and Josephus*, 9, 190, 191; Brandon, *Jesus and the
Zealots*, 25, 65, 145.

56   Charles Gore, *The Epistle to the Romans* (London: John Murray, 1901), 121.

and the temple destroyed by Nebuchadnezzar. The ascendancy of Nebuchadnezzar, as shown previously, was not viewed merely as matter of raw power or the decretive will of God. The pervasive witness of the Old Testament is that Jehovah had transferred to Nebuchadnezzar and his Gentile successors the legitimate civil authority over His people. The detailed proof of these assertions has been presented previously.

This legitimate civil authority over the people of God imparted to Nebuchadnezzar is in Daniel 2 associated with and enlarged to include the Gentile kingdoms that would succeed Nebuchadnezzar until the reestablishment of the theocratic kingdom. Interestingly enough, upon the most likely and common interpretation of the visions of Daniel 2, the fourth of those Gentile kingdoms was the very one of which Paul was speaking in Romans 13:1–7 when he said, "There is no authority except from God, and those which exist are established by God" (v. 1).

This conception of the background of Paul's assertions in Romans 13:1 connects these assertions directly with the problem of theocratically rooted Jewish nationalism. Paul's words amount to a blanket disavowal of and renunciation of the theocratic premises of the Jewish revolutionaries. In direct continuity with the messages of the later prophets, especially Jeremiah, Paul proclaims the disruption of the theocratic kingdom and the transfer of civil authority over God's people to the Gentile kingdoms until its perfected reestablishment under Jesus, the Messiah, at His return in glory.

V. The Intentions and Implication of Verses 3 and 4

A single question directly to do with the thesis of this paper must be answered regarding these verses. Do verses 3 and 4 qualify the requirements of verses 1 and 2?

A number of interpreters particularly in the Reformed tradition utilize verses 3 and 4 as an avenue by which to qualify the apparently absolute demands of verses 1 and 2 and introduce the concept of just rebellion into this passage.[57] Yoder ably summarizes the tenets and history of this interpretation:

> As long as a given government lives up to a certain minimum set of requirements, then that government may properly claim the sanction of divine institution. If, however, a government fails adequately to fulfill the functions divinely assigned to it, it loses its authority. It then becomes the duty of the preacher to teach that this has become an unjust government, worthy of rebellion. It can become the duty of Christian citizens to rise up against it, not because they are against the government but because they are in favor of proper government. The concept of just rebellion, in which the preacher himself does not become a revolutionary but does preach the moral obligation to rise up against unjust government in the name of proper government, finds its rootage in Huldrych Zwingli. In the second generation of the Reformed tradition, the generation of Calvin, it was already being worked out in some detail in its application to the position of the Huguenots in France. It continues through John Knox and Cromwell and through the American Revolution, and is currently being applied in a very consistent way by a particular current of ecumenical thought which would justify the rebellion of subject peoples in Latin America or Africa against white American and Western European cultural and economic imperialism.[58]

---

57   Hodge, *Romans*, 414–415; Reese, "Pauline Politics: Rom. 13:1–7," 331; W. H. G. Thomas, *St Paul's Epistle to the Romans* (Grand Rapids: Eerdmans, 1946), 352.
58   Yoder, *The Politics of Jesus*, 201.

It must be remembered that this use of these verses and the theory of just rebellion itself has been rejected and critiqued from within the Reformed tradition, beginning with Calvin himself.[59] One must begin by clearly stating that it is certainly not Paul's intention in these verses to qualify his foregoing demands. Many considerations might be brought in support of this point. Most simply, one must note the connective with which verse 3 begins. It is "for," not "nevertheless," "however," or "but." Whether this is connected with verse 2b or much more probably with verse 1a,[60] the thought is surely that the considerations to be brought forward in verses 3 and 4 are intended to support or motivate to the demands of the first two verses. This view of the connection is surely confirmed when Paul in verse 5 deduces from verses 3 and 4 (*dio*) the duty of subordination, repeating the verb used in verse 1a (*hupatasso*). Hodge and those in the Reformed tradition who agree with him are, then, certainly not in harmony with the original intention of verses 3 and 4 when they erect a theory of just rebellion upon them.[61] It may be thought barely possible, however, that a legitimate implication of these verses may ultimately lead to the concept of just rebellion. To that slight possibility, we must now turn.

Cranfield well states the larger exegetical question at stake in the interpreting of verses 3 and 4: "Verses 3 and 4 are puzzling. The difficulty is, of course, that Paul seems to take no account of the possibility of the government's being unjust and punishing the good work and praising the evil."[62] This problem is particularly acute when it is remembered that within ten years of the penning of Romans, the church would be engulfed in fiery persecution at the hand of Nero and his successors. Different writers recognize the problem and delineate and discuss the options. Yoder presents

---

59   Calvin, *The Epistle of Paul to the Romans*, 797–806; *The Institutes*, (4:20:24–32).
60   Murray, *The Epistle to the Romans*, 150; Hodge, *Romans*, 407; Denney, *The Expositor's Greek Testament: St. Paul's Epistle to the Romans*, 696.
61   Hodge, *Romans*, 407; Reese, "Pauline Politics: Rom. 13:1–7," 331.
62   Cranfield, "A Commentary on Romans 12–13," 73.

and refutes the "positivist" view (associated with the Lutheran tradition) and the "legitimist" or "normative" view (associated with the Reformed tradition mentioned above), before arguing the case for his own view.[63] Bahnsen refutes at length the "descriptive" view (which he also calls the "positivistic" approach). More briefly, he also rejects the "normative" view (identical with that given the same name by Cranfield above). He is satisfied with neither and combines elements of both in his own view.[64] Cranfield delineates three viewpoints: the experiential, the normative view, and the providential view (his own choice).[65]

It would greatly lengthen and widely deviate from the purpose of this book to adequately state and thoroughly critique each of these viewpoints. The specific concern here is with the normative view, which has characterized many in the Reformed tradition.

As over against the positivist approach that tends to "grant autonomy to the state,"[66] the normative approach certainly embodies an authentic biblical insight. Paul's thought is built on the pattern of Old Testament Wisdom that everywhere subjects the civil authorities to God and His Word. As "ministers" and "servants of God" and His preceptive will, the civil authorities are themselves necessarily subordinate to God's preceptive will.

Paul does not, however, stress this in Romans 13. Further, when the deduction is drawn that failure to conform, at least nominally, to the norm imparts the right of revolution to their subjects, a logical fallacy is committed. Such a deduction must be rejected for the following reasons:

1. The failure of civil authority to conform to the norms of God does not imply the right of subjects to rebel except on the supposition of popular sovereignty. It is just that supposition this passage exposes as incorrect. Civil authority is the

---

63   Yoder, *The Politics of Jesus*, 200ff.

64   Bahnsen, *Theonomy in Christian Ethics*, 366–371.

65   Cranfield, "A Commentary on Romans 12–13," 73.

66   Bahnsen, *Theonomy in Christian Ethics*, 367.

ordinance, minister, and servant of God, not of men, according to Romans 13. The implication is that the authority God has given, only He may take away.

2. The deduction flies in the face of the whole thrust and intention of Paul in Romans 13:1–7. Surely it would be strange if in a passage intended to motivate Christians to subordination to rulers and to the refusal to rebel, Paul would bring forward considerations that would immediately lead to the opposite conclusion!

3. The whole drift of the Bible's teaching is against the concept of just rebellion. To admit the concept in immediate proximity to one of its most emphatic statements of that teaching strains the credibility of any interpretation.

Moving now from this deduction from the normative view to the normative view itself, one must surely observe, first of all, that it severs the connection instituted by Paul between verses 3 and 4 and their context. These verses are encouragement and motivation to obey the existing Roman authorities. If Christians do so, Paul asserts, they will have nothing to fear. The normative view, however, turns the "is" of verse 4a into an "ought to be." It makes Paul say, "For it ought to be a minister of God to you for good." How does this statement encourage a Christian to submit and obey? To say that the Romans should do what is good because their rulers ought to praise them for it is quite obviously no encouragement at all. The Roman authorities ought to reward the good and punish the evil, but who knows if they will? One cannot, therefore, evade the "descriptive" character of verses 3 and 4. The natural reading of these verses is also the exegetically necessary one. Paul is clearly telling us what civil authorities actually do and not merely what they are intended to do.

A better solution is available, one that does justice to both the descriptive emphasis and the normative aspects of Paul's statements. This solution is based on the foundational place the political teaching of Old Testament Wisdom had in Paul's thinking.

This place and its relevance for Romans 13:1–7 has already been documented in this chapter. With many of its political statements, the precise difficulty noted by Cranfield with reference to Romans 13:3–4 may be noted (Cf. Prov 14:35, "The king's favor is toward a servant who acts wisely, but his anger is toward him who acts shamefully"; cf. also Prov 16:13, "Righteous lips are the delight of kings, and he who speaks right is loved"). With reference to such statements, questions similar to those raised about Romans 13 may be asked. Is the king's favor always toward a servant who acts wisely? Are righteous lips always the delight of every king? The answer to such questions must begin by a recognition of the ethical emphasis of such proverbs. Such proverbs are not primarily intended to make assertions about the nature of civil rulers but to encourage wise behavior and righteous speaking in the presence of kings. The assertions about kings come in as motivations and encouragements to such wisdom. They are not absolute promises but general encouragements to wisdom. The non-absolute character of such encouragements (what may be called general promises) can be illustrated widely in the Proverbs (see 10:3, 4, 7; 12:11, 24.)

These promises to the diligent and the righteous may be falsified again and again unless it is understood they state the general tendencies of certain behavior in God s world and not absolute premises. The fact is that civil authority actually is as a general rule what Paul and the book of Proverbs say it is. It *is* this because it has been ordained to be this. Exceptions to the rule do not nullify or frustrate the continuing power of God's ordination of civil authority. It still continues to be what God intended it to be. Similar statements may be made about the institutions of marriage and the Sabbath, though this is not meant to imply that civil government is, like these institutions, a creation ordinance. God blessed the seventh day, the Sabbath (Gen 2:3; Exod 20:11), thus making it effectually a channel of religious blessing to the human race. The fact that to some men it is no blessing does not change the inherent character of the institution or negate its general tendency.

Civil authority is, then, according to its original institution and general tendency, a blessing to the righteous. This is used by Paul in Romans 13 as a reason to submit to its authority. This point must not be missed. Exceptions to this general tendency do not negate the duties it is used to encourage. As Ridderbos perceptively notes, Paul's position is "not founded in the first instance on what is to be expected from the civil authorities, but what one owes than for God's sake."[67] This assertion can be helpfully illustrated from the very proverbs noted earlier. How would it be, for instance, if one argued as follows: I can foresee because I live in a Communist society that it is impossible for me to become rich if I am diligent, therefore it is not my duty to be diligent. Or I can foresee that being righteous will only result in oppression by the wicked, which will result in my family and me being reduced to starvation, therefore I will not be righteous (see Prov 10:3, 7). Exactly analogous is the argument of those who say, "My government does not punish the evil or reward the righteous, therefore I need not subordinate myself to it." Such arguments are clearly perverse and a perversion of the intentions and implications of general encouragements like that of Romans 13:3–4. We must be careful that in finding difficulties with the enforcements we are not objecting to our duty.

Verses 3 and 4 are, then, no escape route for those seeking to evade the Pauline ethic of subordination to civil authority. No such escape route exists. For with respect to the precise issue at stake here—armed rebellion against one's existing civil authorities—Paul's call for subordination is absolute, universal, and unconditional!

---

67   Ridderbos, *Paul*, 322.

Chapter 5

THE THESIS CLARIFIED AND AMPLIFIED

The writer is sensitive to the fact that the thesis he has defended in this book is one that does not commend itself to most minds, even Christian minds, today. Such modern prejudice makes it liable to much misunderstanding and even misrepresentation. The business, therefore, of this concluding chapter will be to obviate these possibilities by clarifying and applying the thesis. This task will, however, be accomplished in an abbreviated fashion because the writer is also conscious that more than sufficient evidence has already been presented in the body of the dissertation for the thesis. Additionally, much of the clarification here to be given will be simply the systematic compilation and brief expansion of remarks made at different places in the dissertation. For these reasons, comparative brevity will characterize this chapter.

I. THE THESIS CLARIFIED

A thoughtful reader will raise a number of questions as to the exact purport of the doctrine that the Bible absolutely forbids all revolution. Several of these questions have generally to do with what constitutes revolution. These will be treated under a single heading.

161

A. The Nature of Revolution

Questions like the following swirl around this issue: Is secession revolutionary? How does a Christian citizen respond to a "civil war"? Is secession revolutionary? When does disobedience become revolution? What civil authorities have the right to lead a revolution? Or, more properly stated, by what civil leadership is the use of armed force legitimated? In other words, what civil authority is necessary to constitute the use of armed force non-revolutionary and, therefore, lawful?

The viewpoint from which such questions must be considered is that of Romans 13:1–7. That passage brings to concentrated expression the perspective of the whole Word of God. As has been shown, that passage requires unqualified subordination to the civil authorities over us within the sphere of their authority and absolutely forbids all armed revolt against them. While such requirements do not prohibit all disobedience, they do forbid all armed assault upon our civil authorities. Given a clear understanding of whom our civil authority is, no question remains as to our duty. But what about this "given"? Several things must here be said.

The Old Testament background and the historical context of Romans 13:1–7 do not permit the question about the legitimacy of existing civil authorities even to be raised. According to the passage, all existing civil authority is established by God and is owed subjection by those placed under it. No exceptions to this duty are allowed on any grounds. Whether those grounds concern the historical origin, the present form, or the moral conduct of the existing civil authority, they are irrelevant as to the question of the duty of subordination to those authorities.

With respect to all this, Romans 13:1–7 allows no question to remain. There is, however, a question not addressed in Romans 13:1–7.[1] In situations of historical flux and political transition, how is a Christian to identify the civil authority to whom he owes his subordination? Paul is not thinking of this question in Romans

---

1   Murray, *The Epistle to the Romans*, 150.

13:1–7 because in his historical milieu, it was not problematic. The fact is that for most of the world, most of the time this question is not at issue. Paul gives no countenance to those in his day or those in ours who, with a lack of biblical sobriety and historical realism, frivolously raise questions as to whom the existing civil authorities are. Let them disobey the law and find out! There are, however, those exceptional historical situations in which legitimate problems may arise as to the identity of one's civil rulers. Such problems are to be resolved by a sensitive application of the general principles of God's Word to the unique political realities of the historical situation. The relevant, biblical principles and the peculiarities of the various historical situations will differ so markedly that it is impossible for the Scriptures or this writer exhaustively to address the question.

It is this question, however, that is strategically involved in many of the questions raised earlier. Those questions provide the opportunity to illustrate helpfully the true purport of the thesis.

Is secession revolutionary? The question here depends entirely on the nature of the civil order existing prior to the (attempted) secession. If the federal or confederate order existing prior to secession was simply a voluntary coalition of sovereign states, as Dabney and other spokesmen for the South viewed the United States of America before the "War between the States," then they were perfectly in harmony with the demand of Romans 13:1–7 when they concluded that their existing civil authority was the State of Virginia.[2] In short, the question here is political and not theological.

How does a Christian citizen or subject respond to civil war? A bewildering multiplicity of specific situations may be imagined here. Generally speaking, it is the Christian's duty to form a just conception of the party to whom political sovereignty belongs on the basis of the preexisting civil order. To that party his political

---

2   Robert Lewis Dabney, *Life and Campaigns of Lieut. Gen. T. J. (Stonewall) Jackson* (Harrisonburg: Sprinkle, 1983), 126ff.

subordination must belong, although the precise degree to which he actively supports in practical ways that party is dependent on other factors. If the Christian finds it impossible to form a clear conviction as to the identity of his civil authorities on the basis of the preexisting civil order, he is at liberty to decide, first, on the basis of biblical and ethical preferences, and then, on the basis of prudential considerations, which party—if any—he will give his support and to what degree.

No matter what decisions the Christian has made in the earlier stages of such a conflict, the time may come in which the Christian must soberly recognize the results of armed force and submit to the orderings of divine providence. At such time, his options are to subordinate himself to the (new) "powers that be," or flight from the country dominated by such "powers" and subordination to the civil authorities of his new country. The covert prolonging of hostilities and armed violence after the public defeat of one's party must be carefully avoided by the Christian in the fear of becoming a thief and murderer in the eyes of God.

What specific civil authorities are sufficient to constitute the use of armed force under their leadership lawful and non-revolutionary? This question has for its historical background the contention of certain in the Reformed tradition that, though all use of armed force must be led by civil magistrates, it is lawful for inferior magistrates to lead a revolution.

Again, this question cannot be answered without consideration of the concrete political order in question. First Peter 2:13–14 makes explicit what seems to the writer to be implicit in Romans 13:1–7: "Submit yourselves for the Lord's sake to every human institution, whether to a king as the one in authority, or to governors as sent by him." As the translation of the NASB brings out, Christians are to subject themselves to governors "as sent by him" (the king), *hos di autou pempomenois*. The thought is apparently that the authority of the governors is derived from the (supreme) authority of the king, and our subordination is due them on that basis and in that way. Palpably, it would be wrong, then, to rise in arms against the king under the leadership of a governor who derives his authority from the king. Likewise, on the basis of Romans 13:1–7, it would be indefensible for the "inferior magistrate" to rise in armed force against his political superiors. Hence, it would be wrong for Christians to follow him in his sin.

The answer, then, must be that to use armed force, one must have some reason to claim that one is or represents the supreme civil authority of a country or, at least, has the right within its political structure to independent action and force. We are thinking in this final phrase of Calvin's much debated "guardians of the people" (*Institutes* 4:20:31). Speaking of Calvin, the answer just given is, of course, the one that Calvin's conscience required him to give again and again in the French situation. As noted in chapter 2, Calvin insisted that only those with some claim to the throne of France could take the lead in any use of armed force.

Another question that needs to be addressed here is this: When does disobedience become revolution? As was pointed out in the introduction to this paper, Romans 13:1–7 assumes a distinction between disobedience and revolution. Just as clearly, it may be asserted on the basis of the foregoing exposition that there are at least two peculiarities of revolution when compared with mere disobedience. First, revolution involves the use of violence, the threat or the actuality of bodily harm. Second, revolution involves the intent of subverting the existing civil authorities and order— that is, destroying it and replacing it with another. The conclusion is simple. Disobedience to government edicts that involves the use of violence or the intent of subversion are revolutionary and unethical.

The final question that must be addressed here is of a slightly different character, but it is convenient to answer it at this point. It is the question of the relation of our thesis to "classic pacifism." It will be sufficient to simply summarize what should be evident by now from the foregoing treatment.

There is a sense in which the question is a natural one, since the advocacy of nonviolence in any sense makes one think of pacifism. Further, it is a fact that classic pacifism is in agreement with our thesis that it is illegitimate for the Christian to engage in violent revolution. The writer welcomes whatever support his thesis may receive from the convictions of the many sincere Christians in this tradition. He is conscious, however, that because of his own Baptist convictions on the subject of ecclesiology, one of a more traditional, Reformed background may be quick to charge the thesis of this thesis with creeping Anabaptism.

It must, therefore, be pointed out that—in light of the exegetical and theological positions adopted and defended within this thesis—it is completely unwarranted to identify the thesis of this dissertation with pacifism or Anabaptism. It is the Reformed doctrine of civil government that is assumed and defended within these pages. That civil government is a divine institution, that a Christian may exercise a civil office, that the civil authorities legitimately exercise the power of the sword including both the death penalty and war on just occasion are all positions maintained by the Reformed tradition and rejected by the Anabaptist tradition. These are the positions advocated in these pages; and they justify its claim to the description *Reformed*. Assuming the treatment of Calvin presented in this thesis to be correct, the charge would be tantamount to the oddity of accusing Calvin himself of creeping Anabaptism!

Finally, the single point at which a similarity between Anabaptism and the thesis of this dissertation exists itself epitomizes its commitment to the distinctively Reformed concept of vocation. The Reformed have always emphasized in their ethical teaching the concept of God-given callings that condition the ethical duty of individuals. The concept of vocation provides an ethical structure most hospitable to our thesis. For the thesis of this dissertation is not that all violence is wrong. That is classic pacifism, but that is not the thesis of this dissertation. The thesis is that violence, armed force, is wrong for the private individual but perfectly legitimate for those whose vocation it is to exercise civil authority. All this is simply a straightforward application of the Reformed doctrine of vocation.

II. THE THESIS APPLIED

A. *Against Modern Reformed Advocacy of Just Revolution*

It is not possible to examine every theory of just revolution being advocated in our day. Neither would it be within the scope or interest of this dissertation. Theories being promulgated outside the Reformed tradition and doctrine of Scripture, for instance, by the so-called Liberation Theologians, will be passed by in order to briefly critique advocacy of the doctrine of just revolution from more respectable sources within the company of contemporary Reformed writers.

This advocacy is coming from two somewhat diverse circles. It is characteristic of "theonomist" writers to adopt the rhetoric of just revolution. Gary North is representative of the typical theonomic adoption of the doctrine of just revolution.[3] On the other hand, Greg Bahnsen in his *Theonomy in Christian Ethics* rejects certain of the typical tenets of this position and fails to make his own position regarding the doctrine of just revolution clear.[4]

Perhaps more well-known than such writers is the advocacy of this position by those in the "Schaeffer" circle. Here we must think of Francis Schaeffer's *Christian Manifesto* and mention also Franky Schaeffer and John W. Whitehead.[5]

These two circles are marked by a certain amount of theological

---

3   Gary North, ed., *The Theology of Christian Resistance* (Tyler, TX: The Geneva Divinity School Press, 1983), xvi, xx, 3–11, 51–64, 102–110, 237, 238, 288–295.

4   Greg Bahnsen, *Theonomy in Christian Ethics* (Phillipsburg: Presbyterian and Reformed, 1984), 366–400.

5   Francis Schaeffer, *A Christian Manifesto* (Westchester: Crossway, 1981), 63–138; Franky Schaeffer, *A Time for Anger; The Myth of Neutrality* (Westchester, Crossway, 1982), 46–54, 122, 150; North, *The Theology of Christian Resistance*; John W. Whitehead, "Christian Resistance in the Face of State Interference," 1–13.

diversity. This becomes clear in Francis Schaeffer's unqualified rejection of theocracy. He says, "We must make definite that we are in no way talking about any kind of theocracy."[6] Such a rejection of theocracy, at least in so unqualified terms, is contrary to the theonomic approach that rejects the separation of church and state in the form Schaeffer would support.[7]

On the matter of just revolution, however, there is apparently considerable unity between these circles. Both circles derive their doctrine from a rediscovery of the political theories of Knox and Rutherford as epitomized in *Lex Rex*.[8] Gary North is happy to enlist Schaeffer and Whitehead in his cause in *The Theology of Christian Resistance*. After his own introduction, North assigns the first two places in his symposium to Whitehead and Schaeffer respectively.[9] Finally, both circles display a typical Calvinistic conservatism as to the actual exercise of their theory of revolution. This is particularly evident in North's introduction to the companion volume to the *Theology of Christian Resistance, The Tactics of Christian Resistance*. In a rather scathing attack on "romantic revolutionaries," North says, "We do not want or need bloodshed in our struggle against the legally constituted government."[10] This is not a rejection of the theory of just revolution but a strategic judgment on his part. As Whitehead says, armed revolution at the present time would be "ill-advised" and "a strategic error," yet he also asserts, "There does come a time when force, even physical force, is appropriate."[11] Both Schaeffer and Whitehead, drawing on Rutherford, stress that several steps must be taken before the resort to armed force and that the use of such force must be defensive in character.[12]

6   Francis Schaeffer, *A Christian Manifesto*, 120.
7   Schaeffer, 121; see also North, *The Theology of Christian Resistance*, 64. There North recommends that Christians work toward the "removal of tax exemption for the liberal denominations, not to mention the cults."
8   Samuel Rutherford, *Lex Rex* (Harrisonburg, VA: Sprinkle, 1982).
9   North, ed., *The Theology of Christian Resistance*. 1–23.
10 Gary North, ed., *The Tactics of Christian Resistance* (Tyler, TX: The Geneva Divinity School Press, 1983), xxxvi.
11 Whitehead, "Christian Resistance in the Face of State Interference," 11.
12 Whitehead., 10, 11; Schaeffer, *A Christian Manifesto*, 103ff., 117.

It is important, however, not to misunderstand what these men mean by *defensive*. Whitehead explains, "This was the situation in the American Revolution. The colonists used force in defending themselves. . . . Note that the colonists did not cross the Atlantic Ocean and mount a physical attack on Great Britain itself. They defended their homeland. As such, *the American Revolution was a conservative counter-revolution.*"[13]

For these reasons and because it very likely is the most well-known book advocating the doctrine of just revolution (North tells us, "Francis Schaeffer s book, *A Christian Manifesto*, replaced one of James Dobson's books as the best-selling Christian book in America in July of 1982"[14]) in our critique of this modern Reformed advocacy of the doctrine of just revolution, *A Christian Manifesto* will be treated as representative.

In critiquing Schaeffer's doctrine of just revolution, one faces several difficulties. Schaeffer moves back and forth from his own thoughts to Rutherford's arguments. We shall work on the assumption that seems to underlie this format, that Schaeffer and Rutherford are of one mind. Another difficulty is that Schaeffer's book is a manifesto, as the title indicates, and not a systematic treatise. Partially for this reason, the relevant sections of the book are written in a very popular style and tend to be somewhat rambling when looked at from a critical point of view. We can only alert the reader of the following criticisms to this fact and assert that the present writer believes his understanding of Schaeffer's assertions to be accurate.

We begin by noting that Schaeffer adopts the normative view of Romans 13:1–7 examined and refuted in the body of this dissertation. He says, for instance, after quoting Romans 13:1–4, "The state is to be an agent of justice, to restrain evil by punishing the wrongdoer, and to protect the good in society. When it does the reverse, *it has no proper authority*. It is then a usurped authority

---

13   Whitehead, "Christian Resistance in the Face of State Interference," 11ff.
14   North, ed., *The Theology of Christian Resistance*, 40.

and as such it becomes lawless and is tyranny."[15] This and much that follows from Rutherford's *Lex Rex* conditions the legitimacy of civil authority and subjection to it on the moral conduct of civil authority. As has been made clear, such a view does not comport with that of the Scriptures or Calvin.

There is something inconsistent or contradictory in the attitude of Schaeffer-Rutherford toward tyrannical government. First, it is argued that "since tyranny is satanic, not to resist it is to resist God—to resist tyranny is to honor God."[16] Yet this resistance is to take place only in a "defensive posture."[17] One would think, however, given the idea that it is everyone's duty to resist tyranny, that one should resist it as thoroughly and consistently and "offensively" as possible. Merely "defensive" resistance logically would be defective obedience. There is, then, something suspiciously illogical about the opting of Schaeffer-Rutherford for merely "defensive" resistance. Is this not an unintentional recognition of the concept of vocation lingering, out of place, in the conscience of Schaeffer-Rutherford? If we have the right and duty of revolution against tyranny, even as private citizens,[18] then by what consistency must we limit this right and duty to "defensive" resistance and force? Is this not an implicit recognition that the vocation of private citizens differs from that of public officials? If it is, then may it not be that this difference in vocation would forbid private citizens—and, indeed, anyone not in possession of political sovereignty—the right of the use of armed force against the "powers that be"?

Furthermore, there is an unjustified ambiguity in the discussion of Schaeffer-Rutherford regarding resistance to civil authority. The word *resistance* is itself ambiguous and never explicitly defined. The universally admitted propriety of civil disobedience slides imperceptibly into a discussion of rebellion, which Schaeffer

---

15   Schaeffer, *A Christian Manifesto*, 91.
16   Schaeffer, 101.
17   Schaeffer, 117.
18   Schaeffer, 97.

assumes to be only another form of disobedience.[19] This equation of disobedience and rebellion without any attempt at justifying it is inexcusable and, in light of the exegetical data presented in this book, false. Yet further, no distinction is made between disobeying because the only alternative is disobeying God (Acts 5:29) and other forms of civil disobedience not absolutely required to avoid violating God's moral law. Note, for instance, Schaeffer's support of the sit-in at an abortion clinic by Covenant Seminary students for which they were arrested and his support of withholding taxes.[20] I am not contending here that all such civil disobedience is wrong. My point is simply that such sliding from one form of civil disobedience to another illustrates Schaeffer's superficial and simplistic justification of all forms of resistance as no different in principle than necessary disobedience to human laws where they would require disobeying God.

It is necessary, however, to take up more specifically Schaeffer's advocacy of tax rebellion. He says, "In our day an illustration for the need of protest is tax money being used for abortion. After all the normal constitutional means of protest had been exhausted, then what could be done? At some point protest could lead some Christians to refuse to pay some portion of their tax money."[21] As noted in the body of this book, such refusal to pay taxes is both historically and biblically a form of rebellion. As such, it is not an option for the Christian. Both in Matthew 22:15f. and Romans 13:6–7, tax moneys are said to be the possession of one's civil government. They are "Caesar's" (Matt 22:21). They are debts— what is "due" (Rom 13:7). We are not at liberty to withhold what belongs to the government because we disapprove of how it may use it. To do this is theft. Just as we may not withhold money we owe to a drunkard because he will use it to get drunk, we may not withhold taxes because we disapprove of how they may be used. Again, it must be pointed out, the key is the concept of vocation.

---

19 Schaeffer, 89–102.
20 Schaeffer, 119ff; 108.
21 Schaeffer, 108.

It is not our responsibility to decide how tax moneys will be spent; and thus, we will not be held responsible for how they are spent. Quite simply, the taxes we owe are not our money.

Perhaps the heart of Schaeffer's commitment to the private use of force is found in the following telling quotation: "As Knox and Rutherford illustrate, however, the proper use of force is not only the province of the state. Such an assumption is born of naivete. It leaves us without sufficient remedy when and if the state takes on totalitarian dimensions."[22] Perhaps this statement sums up many Christians' attachment to the doctrine of just revolution. Without it, they argue, we could do nothing in the face of totalitarianism. Here, at last, we see that the issue is spiritual. This is so because Schaeffer is engaged with all his compatriots in what the Bible calls "fretting":

> Do not fret because of evildoers,
> Be not envious toward wrongdoers. . . .
> Rest in the LORD and wait patiently for Him;
> Do not fret because of him who prospers in his way,
> Because of the man who carries out wicked schemes.
> Cease from anger and forsake wrath;
> Do not fret; it leads only to evildoing.
> For evildoers will be cut off,
> But those who wait for the LORD, they will inherit the land. (Ps 37:1, 7– 9)

No sufficient remedy? What of "entrusting [oneself] to Him who judges righteously" (1 Pet 2:23)? Or the advice, "Let those 'who suffer according to the will of God . . . entrust their souls to a faithful Creator in doing what is right'" (1 Pet 4:19)? The "faithful Creator" and "the one who judges righteously" are sufficient remedy for any totalitarianism. Those can best hope for His intervention who have not by "fretting" given themselves up to the "evildoing" of supposedly just revolutions.

---

22   Schaeffer, 107.

B. To a Near-Historical Political Situation

At the time this is being written, the most pressing practical questions concerning the actual political application of the thesis relate to the crisis in South Africa. The writer is thankful that, while his application of the thesis to that country may be unpopular, it is nonetheless clear cut.

What is the duty of a black South African toward the government that perpetuates the system of apartheid? It is to subordinate himself to that government, render obedience to it where this can be done without violation of the law of God, and pay his taxes. This is the case because no realistic doubt can be entertained as to the authorities who exist in South Africa. If ever one could confidently apply any text to a modern situation, one may apply Romans 13:1 to the black South African: "Let every person be in subjection to the governing authorities. For there is no authority except from God, and those which exist are established by God."

This is not to say that the present South African government is acting morally in its conduct toward black South Africans. It is not to assert that its present denial of suffrage to blacks is just. It is not to adopt the position that its historical origin was blameless. It is only to assert what the biblical data requires us to say—that all such questions are irrelevant to the moral duty of the black South African to subordinate himself to the "powers that be."

Let the black South African peacefully and insistently seek full political suffrage. Let him within the bounds of the law seek an end to apartheid. Let him disobey civil laws where the Word of God demands it. But let him not usurp the sword that God has not given him. Let him remember the words of Calvin, "It is to act like a horse that has broke loose from the reins to attempt more than what our vocation warrants."[23] Runaway horses always do more harm than good to themselves and everybody else in the long run. One example set by the people of the Philippines in

---

23   John Calvin, *Calvin's Selected Works*, ed. by Jules Bonnet and trans. by David Constable (Grand Rapids: Baker, 1983), 6:245–246.

their restraint in the recent political disorders and in the success of their peaceful protest against a tyrant ought to encourage the downtrodden peoples of South Africa and other countries that such restraint is not only pleasing to God but, on the whole, for their own good.

BIBLIOGRAPHY

Abineno, J. L. C. "The State According to Romans Thirteen" In *Southeast Asia Journal of Theology*, XIV (1972), 23–27.

Ackroyd, Peter R. *Exile and Restoration*. Philadelphia: Westminster, 1968.

Alford, Henry. *Alford's Greek New Testament: An Exegetical and Critical Commentary, Volume II, Acts-II Corinthians*. Grand Rapids: Baker Book House, 1980.

Archer, Gleason. *A Survey of Old Testament Introduction*. Chicago: Moody, 1974.

Bahnsen, Greg L. *Theonomy in Christian Ethics*. Phillipsburg, NJ: Presbyterian and Reformed, 1984.

Baldwin, Joyce. *Daniel*. Downers Grove, IL: IVP Academic, 1978.

Baron, Hans. "Calvinist Republicanism and Its Historical Roots" In *Church History*, VIII (1939), 30–42.

Barrett, C. K. *The Epistle to the Romans*. London: A. and C. Black, 1957.

Barrett, C. K. *New Testament Background: Selected Documents*. New York: Harper, 1961.

Barth, Karl, and Will Herberg. *Community, State, and Church*. Garden City, NY: Doubleday, 1960.

Borg, Marcus. "A New Context for Romans 13" In *New Testament Studies*, XIX (January 1973), 205–128.

Boulton, Wayne. "The Riddle of Romans 13." In *The Christian Century*, XCIII (1976), 758–761.

Boutflower, C. *In and Around the Book of Daniel*. Grand Rapids: Zondervan, 1963.

Braaten, Carl E. "Rom. 12:14–21." In *Interpretation*, XXXVIII (July 1984), 291–295.

Brandon, S. G. F. *Jesus and the Zealots*. Manchester: John Rylands Library, 1967.

Bright, John. *A History of Israel*. Philadelphia: Westminster, 1959.

Brown, David. *A Commentary on the Old and New Testaments: Acts–Romans*. Grand Rapids: Eerdmans, 1976.

Brown, Francis; Driver, S. R.; Griggs, Charles A. *Hebrew and English Lexicon of the Old Testament*. Oxford: Clarendon, 1962.

Bruce, F. F. "Paul and the 'powers that be.'" In *The Bulletin of the John Rylands Library*, LXVI (Spring 1984), 78–96.

Calvin, John. *Calvin's Commentaries*, vols. II, V, XII, XIII, XIV, XVI, XVII, XVIII, XIX, XXII. Grand Rapids: Baker Book House, 1981.

———. *Calvin's Selected Works*, vols. IV–VII. ed. by Jules Bonnet, trans. by David Constable. Grand Rapids: Baker Book House, 1983.

———. *The Institutes of the Christian Religion*, trans. by John Allen, 2 vols., 7th ed., Philadelphia, n.d.

———. *Treatises "Against the Anabaptists" and "Against the Libertines,"* ed. and trans. by B. W. Farley. Grand Rapids: Baker Academic, 1982.

Cheneviere, Marc. "Did Calvin Advocate Theocracy?" In *Evangelical Quarterly*, IX (1937), 160–168.

Craigie, Peter C. *The Book of Deuteronomy*. Grand Rapids: Eerdmans, 1976.

Cranfield, C. E. B. "The Christian's Political Responsibility According to the New Testament." In *The Scottish Journal of Theology* (1962), 179–192.

——. *A Commentary on Romans 12–13*. Edinburgh: Oliver & Boyd, 1965.

——. "Some Observations on Rom. 13:1–7." In *New Testament Studies* (April 1960), 241–249.

Culbertson, William and Herman B. Centz. *Understanding the Times*. Grand Rapids: Zondervan, 1956.

Cullman, Oscar. *The State in the New Testament*. London: SCM, 1957.

Culver, Robert D., *Toward a Biblical View of Civil Government*, Chicago, 1974.

Dabney, Robert Lewis. *Life and Campaigns of Lieut. Gen. T.J. (Stonewall) Jackson*. Harrisonburg: Sprinkle, 1983.

Davies, William Davis. *The Setting of the Sermon on the Mount*. Cambridge: Cambridge University Press, 1964.

Davis, John D. *Davis Dictionary of the Bible*, "Theocracy." Grand Rapids, 4th ed., 1954.

Denney, James. *The Expositor's Greek Testament: St. Paul's Epistle to the Romans*, Vol. II, ed. by W. Robertson Nicoll. Grand Rapids: Eerdmans, 1970.

Dooyeweerd, Herman. *The Christian Idea of the State*. Nutley, NJ: Craig, 1968.

Edersheim, Alfred. *Old Testament Bible History*. Wilmington, n.d.

Ehler, Sidney Z. and John B. Morrall. *Church and State Through the Centuries*. London: Burns and Oates, 1954.

Enslin, Morton Scott. *The Ethics of Paul*. New York: Harper & Bros., 1930.

Fairbairn, Patrick. *The Typology of Scripture*. Welwyn, 1975.

Farmer, W. R. *Maccabees, Zealots, and Josephus*. New York: Columbia University, 1957.

Fensham, Frank Charles. *The Books of Ezra and Nehemiah*. Grand Rapids: Eerdmans, 1982.

Forell, George Wolfgang. *The Christian Lifestyle: Reflections on Romans 12–15*. Philadelphia: Fortress, 1975.

Gale, Herbert M. "Paul's View of the State." In *Interpretation*, VI (October 1952), 409–414.

Garrett, James L. "The Dialectic of Rom. 13:1–7 and Revelation 13: Part One." In *The Journal of Church and State*, XVIII (Autumn, 1976), 433–442 and XIX (Winter, 1977), "Part Two," 5–20.

Geldenhuys, Norval. *Commentary on the Gospel of Luke*. Grand Rapids: Eerdmans, 1975.

Girdlestone, Robert Baker. *Synonyms of the Old Testament*. Grand Rapids: Eerdmans, 1976.

Goodenough, Erwin R. *The Politics of Philo Judaeus*. New Haven: Yale University Press, 1938.

Gore, Charles. *St. Paul's Epistle to the Romans*. London: John Murray, 1901.

Gosselin, E. A. "David in Tempore Belli: Beza's David in the Service of the Huguenots." In *Sixteenth Century Journal*, VII (1976), 31–54.

Guggenheim, A. H. "Beza, Viret, and the Church of Nimes." In *Bibliotheque, Humanisme, et Renaissance*, XXXVII (1975), 33–47.

Haldane, Robert. *Romans*. Florida, n.d.

Harrison, Everett F., ed. *Baker's Dictionary of Theology*, "Theocracy." Grand Rapids: Baker Book House, 1960.

Harrison, R. K. *Introduction to the Old Testament*. Grand Rapids: Eerdmans, 1979.

Hering, Jean. *A Good and Bad Government According to the New Testament*. Springfield: Charles C. Thomas, 1954.

Hillerdal, Gunner. "Romans 13 and Luther's Doctrine of 'Two

Kingdoms.'" In *The Lutheran World*, X (January 1963), 10–23.

Hodge, Charles. *A Commentary on Romans*. London: Banner of Truth, 1972.

Holwerda, David E., ed. *Exploring the Heritage of John Calvin*. Grand Rapids: Baker Book House, 1976.

Hughes, Philip E., trans. *The Register of the Company of Pastors of Geneva in the Time of Calvin*, Grand Rapids: Eerdmans, 1966.

Hultgren, Arland J. "Reflections on Romans 13:1–7: Submission to Governing Authorities." In *Dialog*, XV (Autumn, 1976), 263–269.

J. H. M. Salmon, ed. *The French Wars of Religion, How Important Were Religious Factors?* Boston: Heath, 1967.

Jamieson, Robert. *A Commentary Critical, Experimental, and Practical on the Old and New Testaments*, vol. 1. Grand Rapids: Eerdmans, 1976.

Kallas, James. "Rom. XIII:1–7: An Interpolation." In *New Testament Studies*, XI (July 1965), 365–374.

Käsemann, Ernst. *New Testament Questions of Today*. Philadelphia: Fortress, 1969.

Keil, Carl Friedrich. *Commentary on the Old Testament*, vols. II, III, VIII, IX. Grand Rapids: Eerdmans, 1975.

Kennard, Joseph Spencer. *Render to God: A Study of the Tribute Passage*. New York: Oxford University Press, 1950.

Kik, J. Marcellus. *Church and State: The Story of Two Kingdoms*. New York: Nelson, 1963.

Kingdon, Robert M. "Calvinism and Democracy, Some Political Implications of Debates on French Reformed Church Government, 1562–1572." In *American Historical Review*, LXIX (1964), 393–401.

———. *Geneva and Consolidation the French Protestant Movement, 1564–1572*. Madison: University of Wisconsin Press, 1967.

———. "The Political Resistance of the Calvinists in France and the Low Countries." In *Church History*, XXVII (1958), 220–229.

Kingdon, R. M., and R. D. Linder, eds. *Calvin and Calvinism, Sources of Democracy?* Lexington, MA: Heath, 1970.

Kline, Meredith. *Treaty of the Great King.* Grand Rapids: Eerdmans, 1963.

Ladd, George Eldon. *A Theology of the New Testament.* Grand Rapids: Eerdmans, 1974.

Legg, J. "The Christian and Revolution." In *Banner of Truth*, CCXL-VII (1984), 9–17.

Lenski, R. C. H. *Interpretation of St. Paul's Epistle to the Romans.* Minneapolis: Augsburg, 1961.

Leon, Harry Joshua. *The Jews of Ancient Rome.* Philadelphia: The Jewish Publ. Soc. of America, 1960.

Leupold, H. C. *Exposition of Daniel.* Minneapolis, 1961.

Linder, R. D. "Pierre Viret and the Sixteenth Century French Protestant Revolutionary Tradition." In *The Journal of Modern History*, XXXVIII (1966), 125–137.

Little, D. "The Christian and Violence; Some Biblical Perspectives on Violence and the Ministry to Those Who Employ It, Mark 12, Romans 13." In *Church and Society*, LXIV (March–April, 1974), 5–15.

Lloyd-Jones, D. Martyn. *Studies in The Sermon on the Mount.* Grand Rapids: Eerdmans, 1971.

Lloyd, H. A. "Calvin and the Duty of Guardians to Resist." In *Journal of Ecclesiastical History*, XXXII (1981), 65–67.

Locke, John. *A Paraphrase and Notes on the Epistles of St. Paul.* London, 1824.

Lorimer, W. L. "Rom. XIII:3." In *New Testament Studies*, XII (July 1966), 389–391.

Marsden, G. M. "Reforming a Reformed Heritage; Calvinism and Pluralism." In *Reformed Journal,* XXIII (1973), 15–20.

McPheeters, W.M. *International Standard Bible Encyclopedia,* "Theocracy," vol. V. Wilmington, n.d.

Minear, Paul S. *The Obedience of Faith: The Purposes of Paul in the Epistle to the Romans.* Bloomington, 1971.

Morrison, Clinton D. *The Powers That Be: Early Rulers and Demonic Powers in Romans 13:1-7* Naperville: Alec R. Allenson, 1960.

Moulder, James. "Romans 13 and Conscientious Disobedience." In *The Journal of Theology for Southern Africa,* XXI (December 1977), 13–23.

Moule, H. C. G. *The Epistle of St. Paul to the Romans,* ed. by W. Robertson Nicoll. Hartford, n.d.

Mueller, William A. *Church and State in Luther and Calvin.* Nashville: Broadman, 1954.

Murray, John. *Collected Writings of John Murray, Volume III.* Edinburgh: Banner of Truth, 1982.

———. *The Epistle to the Romans.* Grand Rapids, 1968.

———. *Principles of Conduct.* Grand Rapids: Eerdmans, 1957.

North, Gary, ed. *The Theology of Christian Resistance,* Tyler, TX: Geneva Divinity School Press, 1983.

O'Neill, J. C. *Paul's Letter to the Romans.* Harmondsworth: Penguin, 1975.

Oehler, Gustav Friedrich. *Theology of the Old Testament,* trans. by George E. Day, 199. Minneapolis, 1978.

Ogle, Arthur B. "A Look at Mark 12:13–17 and Romans 13:1–7." In *Theology Today,* XXXV (October 1978), 254–264.

Parsons, Wilfrid. "The Influence of Romans 13 on Christian Political Thought: 2, Augustine to Hincmar." In *Theological Studies,* II (1941), 328–331.

———. "The Influence of Romans 13 on Pre-Augustinian Christian Political Thought." In *Theological Studies* (December 1940), 337–364.

Pauck, Wilhelm., "Calvin and Butzer." In *The Journal of Religion*, IX (1929), 237–256.

Poole, Matthew. *A Commentary on the Holy Bible*, vols. I, III. London: Banner of Truth, 1974.

Quanbeck, Warren A., ed. *God and Caesar, A Christian Approach to Social Ethics*. Minneapolis: Augsburg, 1959.

Ramsey, Sir William Mitchell. *The Church in the Roman Empire*. New York: Putnam, 1912.

Reese, Boyd. "The Rights of a Citizen." In *The Other Side*, VII (September–October 1971), 13–15.

Reese, T. J. "Pauline Politics' Rom. 13:1–7." In *Biblical Theology Bulletin*, III (October 1973), 323–331.

Ridderbos, Herman. *The Coming of the Kingdom*, trans. by H. deJongste. Philadelphia: Presbyterian and Reformed, 1975.

———. *Paul*. Grand Rapids: Eerdmans, 1975.

Robertson, O. Palmer. *The Christ of the Covenants*. Grand Rapids: Baker Book House, 1980.

Rutherford, Samuel. *Lex Rex*. Harrisonburg, VA: Sprinkle, 1982.

Sabath, R. A. "Paul's View of the State (Romans 13)." In *The Post–American*, III (April 1974), 8–11; (May 1974), 20–22.

Sanday, William and Arthur Headlam. *The Epistle to the Romans*, Edinburgh: T&T Clark, 1952.

Schaeffer, Francis. *A Christian Manifesto*. Westchester: Crossway, 1981.

Schaeffer, Franky. *A Time for Anger: The Myth of Neutrality*. Westchester: Crossway, 1982.

Schultz, A. C. *Zondervan Pictorial Encyclopedia*, "Theocracy," vol. V. Grand Rapids: Zondervan, 1975.

Seitz, O. J. F. "Love Your Enemies." In *New Testament Studies*, XVI (1969–1970), 49–52.

Skinner, Quentin. *The Foundations of Modern Political Thought*, vol. 2. London: Cambridge University Press, 1978.

Starkey, L. M. "Revolution, Religion, and Romans." In *Religion in Life*, XLII (Autumn 1973), 334–343.

Stein, Peter. "Calvin and the Duty of Guardians to Resist: A Comment." In *Journal of Ecclesiastical History*, XXXII (1981), 69,70.

Stevick, D. B., *Civil Disobedience and the Christian*, New York, 1969.

Stringfellow, William. *Conscience and Obedience: The Politics of Romans 13 and Revelation 13 in Light of the Second Coming*. Waco, TX: Word, 1977.

———. *The Politics of Spirituality*. Eugene, OR: Wipf and Stock, 1984.

———. "Watergate and Romans 13." In *Christianity in Crisis*, XXXIII (June 1973), 110–112.

Sutherland, N. M. *The Huguenot Struggle for Recognition*. New Haven: Yale University Press, 1980.

Taylor, William M. *Ruth the Gleaner and Esther the Queen*. New York: George H. Doran, 1919.

Thomas, W. H. Griffith. *St. Paul's Epistle to the Romans*. Grand Rapids: Eerdmans, 1976.

Ullmann, Walter. "Calvin and the Duty of Guardians to Resist: A Comment." In *Journal of Ecclesiastical History*, XXXII (1981), 449–501.

VanderMolen, Ronald. "Political Calvinism." In *The Journal of Church and State*, XI (1969), 457–463.

Von Orelli, C. *The Prophecies of Jeremiah*. Minneapolis, 1977.

Vos, Geerhardus. *Biblical Theology*. Grand Rapids: Eerdmans, 1948.

———. *Pauline Eschatology*, Grand Rapids: Eerdmans, 1972.

Walker, Williston. *John Calvin*. New York: G.P. Putnam's Sons, 1906.

Waskey, Andrew Jackson L., "John Calvin's Theory of Political Obligation: An Examination of the Doctrine of Civil Disobedience and Its Limits from the New Testament Commentaries, University of Southern Mississippi." PhD diss., University of Southern Mississippi, 1987.

Watson, Philip S. *The State as a Servant of God: A Study of its Nature and Tasks*, London: London Society for Promoting Christian Knowledge. 1946.

Webster, Alexander, F. C. "St. Paul's Political Advice to the Haughty, Gentile Christians in Rome: An Exegesis of Rom. 13:1–7." In *St. Vladimir's Theological Quarterly*, XXV (1981), 259–282.

Wigram, George V., ed. *The New Englishman's Hebrew and Chaldee Concordance*. Wilmington, DE: Associated Publishers & Authors, 1975.

Wilson, Geoffrey B. *Romans: A Great Digest of Reformed Comment*. Edinburgh: Banner of Truth, 1977.

Wood, Leon. *A Commentary on Daniel*. Grand Rapids: Zondervan, 1976.

———. *A Survey of Israel's History*. Grand Rapids: Zondervan, 1970.

Yoder, John H. *The Politics of Jesus*. Grand Rapids: Eerdmans, 1972.

Young, Edward J. *The Prophecy of Daniel*. Grand Rapids: Eerdmans, 1949.

Zens, Jon. "Romans 13: Why Did Paul Talk About the State?" In *Searching Together*, XIII (Winter, 1984), 26–27.

Christ Precious to Those Who Believe

John Fawcett

Written in 1799, *Christ Precious to Those Who Believe: The preciousness of Jesus Christ, to those who believe—practically considered and improved* by John Fawcett is a "minor spiritual classic of the eighteenth century that deserves to be better known."

On Your Heart: A Three-Year Devotional for Families

A.J. Genco

On Your Heart is a guide for family worship based on a three-year cycle. It provides both Scripture passages to read and discussions questions to ask for each of the nearly 1100 days in the cycle. At the end of three years, you and your family will have read through and discussed the entire Bible together.

Let the Little Children Come: Family Worship on Sundays (And the Other Six Days Too)

Scott Aniol

"This is a book you can use every day of your child-raising years. Your children will be gone sooner than you think; if you use this book as your guide, you will be glad you did. Don't let the opportunity slip away."

– Scott Brown, Pastor, Hope Baptist Church, Wake Forest, NC; President, Church and Family Life

Christian Duties

Zenas Trivett

Christian Duties, originally entitled *Plain Christian Duties Recommended*, is an address Zenas Trivett gave at the establishment of a new Baptist congregation in 1791, in which he lays out the various responsibilities of a faithful member of a local church.

The Failure of Natural Theology: A Critical Appraisal of the
Philosophical Theology of Thomas Aquinas

Jeffrey D. Johnson

> "Johnson's scholarly but gracefully readable text shows that his intellect
> notwithstanding, Aquinas's mingled metaphysics, mixed methodology,
> and promotion of "divine immobility" merit strong caution. This is the
> book the church has needed on this subject. It is an urgent read by one
> of our best theologians."
>
> —Dr. Owen Strachan

The Missionary Crisis: Five Dangers Plaguing Missions and How the
Church Can Be the Solution

Paul Snider

> The Missionary Crisis confronts five dangers facing missionaries and the
> local churches that send them and gives biblical and practical instruction
> for missionaries, sending churches, and mission organizations. This book
> boldly approaches gentle correction for the missionary to reverse these
> five crises in their ministries. It challenges the local church to prepare
> and equip men and women for the high calling of missionary life.

Seven Thoughts Every Christian Ought to Think Every Day:
Laying a Foundation for a Life of Prayer

Jim Scott Orrick

> "Searching for great resources to disciple new believers can be like
> Goldilocks tasting porridge. Too difficult, and it frustrates; too fluffy,
> and it misleads. Jim Orrick has that much sought-after gift of taking
> deep truths and bringing the tray to the common man. When a book
> can be handed to an unbeliever for evangelism, read through with a new
> believer to disciple, worked through with the family for worship, and
> also delight the soul of the seasoned in Christ, it is a helpful book."
>
> – Josh Lagrange, Church planter

Basic Christian Doctrines

Dr. Curt Daniel

> "Usually, other attempts to accomplish a work like this fall flat. Either the subjects are treated with far too much verbiage—thus unnecessarily lengthening the prose, or they are easy enough to read but are much too elementary in content. Daniel, however, deftly succeeds with both aims where many other writers do not."
>
> – Dr. Lance Quinn
> Executive Vice-President,
> The Expositors Seminary, Jupiter, FL

The Gospel Made Clear to Children

Jennifer Adams

> "The highest recommendation I can give to this wonderful book is that I will be reading it over and over again to my children. It is rich in biblical doctrine and is an invaluable instrument to aid parents in teaching their children the glorious truths of "God in Christ" reconciling the world to Himself. I know of no other book that so clearly communicates the great doctrines of the gospel to children."
>
> – Paul Washer,
> Author, Director of HeartCry Missionary Society

Ten Essential Sermons of Charles Spurgeon

> "The effort to isolate ten influential sermons from a preacher who preached thousands of such sermons is daunting. These sermons, however, succeed in illustrating Spurgeon's doctrine, his evangelistic commitment, the beauty of his language, the manner in which a biblical text suggests a subject, and his passion for the glory of the triune God and the eternal well-being of souls."
>
> – from the introduction by Tom Nettles

Saving Natural Theology from Thomas Aquinas

Jeffrey D. Johnson

> In this much-anticipated follow-up to *The Failure of Natural Theology*, Jeffrey D. Johnson seeks to separate the reality of natural theology from the Greek philosophy-laden counterfeit advanced by Thomas Aquinas and others. Ultimately, Johnson shows in S*aving Natural Theology from Thomas Aquinas* that if natural theology can be saved (and he believes it can be), it must be saved from Thomas Aquinas.

The Confessing Baptist: Essays on the Use of Creeds in Baptist Faith and Life

Robert Gonzales Jr.

> A growing number of Baptist churches today are rediscovering their confessional heritage. The contributors to this book welcome this rediscovery. Indeed, they hope it continues! With that end in view, they have written and compiled these essays to celebrate and commend the use of creeds and confessions in Baptist faith and life. The primary audiences they have in view are local church leaders and members because sound theology is not just the province of the academy but is essential to the health and ministry of the local church.

Biblical Foundations of Corporate Worship

Scott Aniol

> "Every person responsible for shaping and leading corporate worship should read this book with a serious intent of allowing its arguments and its presentation of examples be considered seriously as a matter of conscience. Christian congregations will find their times together as God-centered, Word-centered, gospel-centered persuasives to conviction, confession, assurance, holiness, and witness."
>
> – Tom J. Nettle
> Professor Emeritus
> The Southern Baptist Theological Seminary

CPSIA information can be obtained
at www.ICGtesting.com
Printed in the USA
LVHW041044250322
714381LV00015B/675

9 781952 599491